ALL

DAY LONG

AN ANTHOLOGY OF POETRY FOR CHILDREN

ALL DAY LONG

compiled by
PAMELA WHITLOCK

with wood engravings by
JOAN HASSALL

LONDON
OXFORD UNIVERSITY PRESS

Oxford University Press, Ely House, London W. 1

GLASGOW NEW YORK TORONTO MELBOURNE WELLINGTON
CAPE TOWN SALISBURY IBADAN NAIROBI DAR ES SALAAM LUSAKA ADDIS ABABA
BOMBAY CALCUTTA MADRAS KARACHI LAHORE DACCA
KUALA LUMPUR SINGAPORE HONG KONG TOKYO

First published 1954
Reprinted 1957, 1958, 1963, 1968, 1970

PRINTED IN GREAT BRITAIN

Contents

IV. *Dream*

V. *Daybreak*

VI. *Very Early*

VII. *Invitations*

VIII. *The Day's Play*

IX. *Solitude*

PART TWO: MORNING GLORY

I. *London Town*

IX. *Let it Rain*

X. *Snowflake and Fall*

PART THREE: AFTERNOON'S AMAZEMENT

I. *The World of People*

II. *Travellers*

xiii

IV. *Play and Puzzle*

V. *Tales, Marvellous Tales*

Acknowledgements

W. H. AUDEN: Mr W. H. Auden; *Some Poems*, 1940; Faber & Faber, Ltd.; the General Post Office.

BARBARA BAKER: Mrs Barbara Baker.

MAURICE BARING: The Executrix of Maurice Baring; *Collected Poems*; William Heinemann Ltd.

HILAIRE BELLOC: *Sonnets & Verse*, 1938; Gerald Duckworth & Co., Ltd.

JOHN BETJEMAN: Mr John Betjeman; *Selected Poems*, 1948; John Murray, Ltd.

LAURENCE BINYON: Mrs Cicely Binyon; The Society of Authors; *Collected Poems of Laurence Binyon*.

GORDON BOTTOMLEY: *Poems of Thirty Years*; Constable & Co., Ltd.

LILIAN BOWES LYON: The Executors of Lilian Bowes Lyon; *The Collected Poems*; Jonathan Cape, Ltd.

RUPERT BROOKE: *The Poetical Works of Rupert Brooke*; Sidgwick & Jackson, Ltd.

ROBERT BRIDGES: *The Shorter Poems of Robert Bridges*; the Clarendon Press.

GERALD BULLETT: *News from the Village*; Cambridge University Press.

ROY CAMPBELL: Mr Roy Campbell; *The Flaming Terrapin*; Jonathan Cape, Ltd.

FRANCES CHESTERTON: Miss D. E. Collins.

G. K. CHESTERTON: Miss D. E. Collins; *The Wild Knight*; J. M. Dent & Sons, Ltd. *Lepanto*; Burns, Oates & Washbourne, Ltd.

RICHARD CHURCH: Mr Richard Church; *Collected Poems*; J. M. Dent & Sons, Ltd.

MARY COLERIDGE: Captain Francis Newbolt; *The Poems of Mary Coleridge*; Rupert Hart-Davis, Ltd.

W. H. DAVIES: Mrs W. H. Davies; *Collected Poems*; Jonathan Cape, Ltd.

GEOFFREY DEARMER: Mr Geoffrey Dearmer.

PAUL DEHN: Mr Paul Dehn; *The Day's Alarm*; Hamish Hamilton, Ltd.

WALTER DE LA MARE: Mr Walter de la Mare; *Collected Poems*; Faber & Faber, Ltd.

JOHN DRINKWATER: *Collected Poems*; Sidgwick & Jackson, Ltd.

IRENE MCLEOD: Miss Irene McLeod.

LOUIS MACNEICE: Mr Louis MacNeice; *Collected Poems*; Faber & Faber, Ltd.

JOHN MASEFIELD: Dr John Masefield, O.M.; The Society of Authors; *Collected Poems*; William Heinemann, Ltd.

CHARLOTTE MEW: Mrs Alida Monro: *The Farmer's Bride; The Rambling Sailor.*

ALICE MEYNELL: Sir Francis Meynell; *The Poems of Alice Meynell*; Oxford University Press.

HAROLD MONRO: Mrs Alida Monro; *Collected Poems.*

T. STURGE MOORE: Mrs Sturge Moore; *The Poems of T. Sturge Moore*, Collected Edition, Vol. I, page 141. Macmillan & Co., Ltd.

J. B. MORTON: Mr J. B. Morton (Beachcomber of the *Daily Express*); *The Dancing Cabman and other Verses*; Frederick Muller, Ltd.

EDWIN MUIR: Mr Edwin Muir; *Collected Poems*; Faber & Faber, Ltd.

OGDEN NASH: Mr Ogden Nash; *Family Reunion*; J. M. Dent & Sons, Ltd.

E. NESBIT: Mr John Farquharson; *The Rainbow and the Rose*; Longmans, Green & Co., Ltd.

ROBERT NICHOLS: Mr Milton Waldman; *Such was my Singing*.

ALFRED NOYES: Mr Alfred Noyes; *Collected Poems*; William Blackwood & Sons, Ltd.

WILFRED OWEN: *The Poems of Wilfred Owen*; Chatto & Windus, Ltd.

RUTH PITTER: Miss Ruth Pitter; *Urania*; The Cresset Press, Ltd.

JOHN PUDNEY: Mr John Pudney; *Dispersal Point*; John Lane the Bodley Head, Ltd.

JAMES REEVES: Mr James Reeves; *The Wandering Moon*; William Heinemann, Ltd.

MICHAEL ROBERTS: Mrs Michael Roberts; *Poems, 1936*; Jonathan Cape, Ltd.

W. R. RODGERS: Mr W. R. Rodgers; *Awake: and other Poems*; Martin Secker & Warburg, Ltd.

V. SACKVILLE-WEST: Miss V. Sackville-West; *Collected Poems*; The Hogarth Press, Ltd.

SIEGFRIED SASSOON: Mr Siegfried Sassoon; *Collected Poems*; Faber & Faber, Ltd.

IAN SERRAILLIER: Mr Ian Serraillier; *Thomas and the Sparrow*; Oxford University Press.

EDWARD SHANKS: Mrs Edward Shanks; *Poems, 1912–32*; Macmillan & Co., Ltd.

Only the Beginning

IT is in moments of excitement that everyday things turn into poetry. Ordinary people like you and me can recognize these moments; here there gone; but try as we do to catch them, they always slip away. It is only the poets who, in their craftily chosen words and rhythms, can make traps and spring them round some of the best and most elusive things. But we can, by just reading or listening, let out again for ourselves from their lines excitements that we feared had vanished for ever.

The poems and verses in this book have been chosen because in each there lies—or so it seemed to me—some exciting thing. You may not, when you first come to each entry, always recognize it. Words must mean slightly different things to each one of us, and different emotions fit into different lives. But an anthology is an easy hopscotch ground and you can quickly skip on to something that does excite you. On another day you may come back to the same book and find yourself jumping through it on quite different stones.

Poetry cannot be kept neatly inside a book or even to certain hours of the day. Prey for poets lies about everywhere in all our most ordinary days. Any moment an amazement may easily turn up. So this book is arranged in the shape of a whole day. It might have as a sub-title, 'The Hut Book', or 'The Cupboard Under The Stairs Book', or 'The Branch Of A Tall Tree Book', because it is not a book of poems for reciting out loud to a roomful of relations, but for reading when you are in a private place with special people, or for sipping secretly when you are alone.

All Day Long is only the beginning of an anthology. It does not attempt to give a balanced picture of the long landscape of English poetry; whole areas and 'complete works' have been missed. Even those poets whose work does appear are unfairly represented; the greatest, particularly, are given much less than their due. Poems that you are likely to meet in literature classes or elsewhere have been left out to leave room for the more recent and the less well known. More poetry of the twentieth century than of any other is included. My reading has been haphazard; luck, more than steady study, has brought this much my way. To share delight, here it is put in yours.

All Day Long is only the beginning of an anthology. More than anything it could be called a collection of gaps. To fill these you must move swiftly on to more comprehensive, more wisely compiled volumes, and to each poet's own works. To make you want to explore further, to hint at what is to be found, is what this book may do. You will not like all of it. When you leave it behind, take with you just those poems that have pleased and excited *you*. It is with these that you will be able to start the only anthology that would have delight breaking out for you on every single page; the one that you make yourself. It could be much bigger and better than this. It could be a most marvellous book. This, then, is only a beginning.

THE EARLY HOURS

I
MIDNIGHT
BEGINS ALL DAYS

1. Sonnet to Sleep

O soft embalmer of the still midnight,
  Shutting, with careful fingers and benign,
Our gloom-pleas'd eyes, embower'd from the light,
  Enshaded in forgetfulness divine;
O soothest Sleep! if so it please thee, close,
  In midst of this thine hymn, my willing eyes,
Or wait the amen, ere thy poppy throws
  Around my bed its lulling charities;
Then save me, or the passed day will shine
Upon my pillow, breeding many woes;
  Save me from curious conscience, that still lords
Its strength for darkness, burrowing like a mole;
  Turn the key deftly in the oiled wards,
And seal the hushed casket of my soul.

JOHN KEATS

2. The Night

Most holy Night, that still dost keep
The keys of all the doors of sleep,
To me when my tired eyelids close
    Give thou repose.

And let the far lament of them
That chaunt the dead day's requiem
Make in my ears, who wakeful lie,
    Soft lullaby.

Let them that guard the horned moon
By my bedside their memories croon.
So shall I have new dreams and blest
    In my brief rest.

Fold thy great wings about my face,
Hide dawning from my resting-place,
And cheat me with your false delight,
    Most Holy Night.

HILAIRE BELLOC

3. From *The Sleep*

Of all the thoughts of God that are
Borne inward unto souls afar,
Along the Psalmist's music deep,
Now tell me if that any is,
For gift or grace, surpassing this—
'He giveth His belovèd sleep'?

II

What would we give to our beloved?
The hero's heart, to be unmoved,
The poet's star-tuned harp, to sweep,
The patriot's voice, to teach and rouse,
The monarch's crown, to light the brows?—
'He giveth *His* belovèd, sleep.'

ELIZABETH BARRETT BROWNING

4. *Night Song*

Sleep, our lord, and for thy peace
    Let thy mother's softer voice
Pray thy patrons to increase
    Freedom from all light and noise.
Hark, her invocation draws
To thy guard those princely Laws!

Prince of Fire, in favour quench
　　Moonlight upon wall and floor;
And with gentle shadow drench
　　Candles entering at the door;
Michael, round about his bed
Be thy great protection shed.

Prince of Air, lest winds rush by
　　Blustering about the park
Of this night, with watchful eye
　　Keep the palings of the dark;
Raphael, round about his bed
Be thy great protection shed.

Prince of Water, if thy rains
　　Must tonight prevent our dearth,
Keep them from the window-panes,
　　Softly let them bless the earth;
Gabriel, round about his bed
Be thy great protection shed.

Prince of Earth, beneath our tread
　　And above each doubtful board
Be thy silent carpet spread;
　　Let thy stillness hush our lord;
Auriel, round about his bed
Be thy great protection shed.

Let your vast quaternion,
　　Earth and Water, Fire and Air,
Friend him as he goes upon
　　His long journey, out to where,
Princes, round his final bed
Be your great protection shed.

CHARLES WILLIAMS

5. Hands

Now rest in abeyance
From market and mill
Millions of hands
Unaware of their skill;
Hands pale as faience,
Hands brown as hazel,
How can I praise all
Those that are gifted?
Hands like the rose
To the wild rose grafted,
How from such good
Can I choose?
Some, lovely food
Have spicily garnished
(Sauces and stews);
Others, nail-varnished,
Have tapped like the yaffle
A texture of news.

Now sleep-arrested
They lie on the pillow,
Or clasped in a fellow,
Or open, uncurled;
And some are as shell-pink
As the silk petals
Of roses unfurled,
The soft hands of children,
The hope of the world.

GEOFFREY DEARMER

6. Old Cat Care

Outside the Cottage

Green-eyed Care
May prowl and glare
And poke his snub, be-whiskered nose:

But door fits tight
Against the Night:
Through criss-cross cracks no evil goes.

Window is small:
No room at all
For Worry and Money, his shoulder-bones:
Chimney is wide,
But Smoke's inside
And happy Smoke would smother his moans.

Be-whiskered Care
May prowl out there:
But I never heard
He caught the Blue Bird.

RICHARD HUGHES

II
BY THE LIGHT
OF THE MOON

1. From *On Leaping Over the Moon*

As if it had ev'n twenty thousand faces,
  It shines at once in many places;
    To all the earth so wide
    God doth the stars divide
      With so much art
      The moon impart,
They serve us all; serve wholly ev'ry one
  As if they served him alone.
While ev'ry single person hath such store,
  'Tis want of sense that makes us poor.

THOMAS TRAHERNE

2. *The Horseman*

I heard a horseman
  Ride over the hill;
The moon shone clear,
The night was still;
His helm was silver,
  And pale was he;
And the horse he rode
  Was of ivory.

WALTER DE LA MARE

3. *Fragments on a Theme*

The silence of a City, how awful at Midnight!
Mute as the battlements and crags and towers
That Fancy makes in the clouds, yea, as mute
As the moonlight that sleeps on the steady vanes.

The cell of a departed anchoret,
His skeleton and flitting ghost are there,
Sole tenants—
And all the City silent as the Moon
That steeps in quiet light the steady vanes
Of her huge temples.

SAMUEL TAYLOR COLERIDGE

4. *Will You Come?*

Will you come?
Will you come?
Will you ride
So late
At my side?
O, will you come?

Will you come?
Will you come
If the night
Has a moon,
Full and bright?
O, will you come?

Would you come?
Would you come
If the noon
Gave light,
Not the moon?
Beautiful, would you come?

Would you have come?
Would you have come
Without scorning,
Had it been
Still morning?
Beloved, would you have come?

If you come
Haste and come.
Owls have cried;
It grows dark
To ride.
Beloved, beautiful, come.

EDWARD THOMAS

5. *Full Moon*

She was wearing the coral taffeta trousers
Someone had brought her from Isfahan,
And the little gold coat with the pomegranate blossoms,
And the coral-hafted feather fan;
And she ran down a Kentish lane in the moonlight,
And skipped in the pool of the moon as she ran.

She cared not a rap for all the big planets,
For Betelgeuse or Aldebaran,
And all the big planets cared nothing for her,
That small impertinent charlatan,
As she climbed on a Kentish stile in the moonlight,
And laughed at the sky through the sticks of her fan.

V. SACKVILLE-WEST

6. *Night-song in the Jungle*

Now Rann the Kite brings home the night
    That Mang the Bat sets free—
The herds are shut in byre and hut,
    For loosed till dawn are we.
This is the hour of pride and power,
    Talon and tush and claw.
Oh hear the call!—Good hunting all
    That keep the Jungle Law!

RUDYARD KIPLING

III

SEEING
THE STARS

1. New Year's Chimes

What is the song the stars sing?
(*And a million songs are as song of one.*)
This is the song the stars sing:
(*Sweeter song's none*)

One to set, and many to sing,
(*And a million songs are as song of one*)
One to stand, and many to cling,
The many things, and the one Thing,
The one that runs not, the many that run.

The ever new weaveth the ever old,
(*And a million songs are as song of one*)
Ever telling the never told;
The silver saith, and the said is gold,
And done ever the never done.

The Chase that's chased is the Lord of the chase,
(*And a million songs are as song of one*)
Colours unseen by the colours seen,
And sounds unheard heard sounds between,
And a night is in the light of the sun.

An ambuscade of light in night,
(*And a million secrets are but as one*)
And a night is dark in the sun's light,
And a world in the world man looks upon.

Hidden stars by the shown stars' wings,
(*And a million cycles are but as one*)
And a world with unapparent strings
Knits the simulant world of things;
Behold, and vision thereof is none.

The world above is the world below,
(*And a million worlds are but as one*)
And the One in all; as the sun's strength so
Strives in all strength, glows in all glow
Of the earth that wits not, and man thereon.

Braced in its own fourfold embrace
(*And a million strengths are as strength of one*)
And round it all God's arms of grace,
The world, so as the Vision says,
Doth with great lightning-tramples run.

And thunder bruiteth into thunder,
(*And a million sounds are as sound of one*)
From stellate peak to peak is tossed a voice of wonder,
And the height stoops down to the depths thereunder,
And sun leans forth to his brother-sun.

And the more ample years unfold
(*With a million songs as song of one*)
A little new of the ever old,
A little told of the never told,
Added act of the never done.

Loud the descant, and low the theme,
(*A million songs are as song of one*)
And the dream of the world is dream in dream,
But the one Is is, or nought could seem;
And the song runs round to the song begun.

This is the song the stars sing,
(*Tonèd all in time*)
Tintinnabulous, tuned to ring
A multitudinous-single thing
(Rung all in rhyme).

FRANCIS THOMPSON

2. *The Starlight Night*

Look at the stars! look, look up at the skies!
  O look at all the fire-folk sitting in the air!
  The bright boroughs, the circle-citadels there!
Down in dim woods the diamond delves! the elves'-eyes!

The grey lawns cold where gold, where quickgold lies!
  Wind-beat whitebeam; airy abeles set on a flare!
  Flake-doves sent floating forth at a farmyard scare!—
Ah well! it is a purchase, all is a prize.

Buy then! bid then!—What?—Prayer, patience, alms, vows.
Look, look! a May-mess, like on orchard boughs!
  Look! March-bloom, like on mealed-with-yellow sallows!
These are indeed the barn; withindoors house
The shocks. This piece-bright paling shuts the spouse
  Christ home, Christ and his mother and all his hallows.

GERARD MANLEY HOPKINS

3. *When I Heard the Learn'd Astronomer*

When I heard the learn'd astronomer,
When the proofs, the figures, were ranged in columns
  before me,
When I was shown the charts and diagrams, to add, divide, and
  measure them,
When I sitting heard the astronomer where he lectured with
  much applause in the lecture-room,
How soon unaccountable I became tired and sick,
Till rising and gliding out I wander'd off by myself,
In the mystical moist night-air, and from time to time,
Look'd up in perfect silence at the stars.

WALT WHITMAN

4. *A Novelty*

Why should I care for the Ages
    Because they are old and grey?
To me, like sudden laughter,
    The stars are fresh and gay;
The world is a daring fancy,
    And finished yesterday.

Why should I bow to the Ages
　　Because they were drear and dry?
Slow trees and ripening meadows
　　For me go roaring by,
A living charge, a struggle
　　To escalade the sky.

The eternal suns and systems,
　　Solid and silent all,
To me are stars of an instant,
　　Only the fires that fall
From God's good rocket, rising
　　On this night of carnival.

G. K. CHESTERTON

5. *Canis Major*

The great Overdog,
That heavenly beast
With a star in one eye,
Gives a leap in the east.

He dances upright
All the way to the west
And never once drops
On his forefeet to rest.

I'm a poor underdog,
But tonight I will bark
With the great Overdog
That romps through the dark.

ROBERT FROST

6. *Wanderers*

Wide are the meadows of night,
And daisies are shining there,
Tossing their lovely dews,
Lustrous and fair;

And through these sweet fields go,
Wand'rers 'mid the stars—
Venus, Mercury, Uranus, Neptune,
Saturn, Jupiter, Mars.

'Tired in their silver, they move,
And circling, whisper and say,
Fair are the blossoming meads of delight
Through which we stray.

WALTER DE LA MARE

7. *Star-talk*

'Are you awake, Gemelli,
  This frosty night?'
'We'll be awake till reveille,
Which is Sunrise,' say the Gemelli,
'It's no good trying to go to sleep:
If there's wine to be got we'll drink it deep,
  But sleep is gone for tonight,
  But sleep is gone for tonight.'

'Are you cold too, poor Pleiads,
  This frosty night?'
'Yes, and so are the Hyads:
See us cuddle and hug,' say the Pleiads,
'All six in a ring: it keeps us warm:
We huddle together like birds in a storm:
  It's bitter weather tonight,
  It's bitter weather tonight.'

'What do you hunt, Orion,
  This starry night?'
'The Ram, the Bull and the Lion,
And the Great Bear,' says Orion,
'With my starry quiver and beautiful belt
I am trying to find a good thick pelt
  To warm my shoulders tonight,
  To warm my shoulders tonight.'

'Did you hear that, Great She-bear,
    This frosty night?'
'Yes, he's talking of stripping *me* bare,
Of my own big fur,' says the She-bear.
'I'm afraid of the man and his terrible arrow:
The thought of it chills my bones to the marrow,
    And the frost so cruel tonight!
    And the frost so cruel tonight!'

'How is your trade, Aquarius,
    This frosty night?'
'Complaints is many and various,
And my feet are cold,' says Aquarius,
'There's Venus objects to the Dolphin-scales,
And Mars to Crab-spawn found in my pails,
    And the pump has frozen tonight,
    And the pump has frozen tonight.'

ROBERT GRAVES

IV
DREAM

1. From *Dream-pedlary*

If there were dreams to sell,
    What would you buy?
Some cost a passing bell;
    Some a light sigh,
That shakes from Life's fresh crown
Only a roseleaf down.
If there were dreams to sell,
Merry and sad to tell,
And the crier rung the bell,
    What would you buy?

    .   .   .   .   .

But there were dreams to sell,
    Ill didst thou buy;
Life is a dream, they tell,
    Waking, to die.
Dreaming a dream to prize,
Is wishing ghosts to rise;
    And, if I had the spell
    To call the buried, well,
        Which one would I?

    .   .   .   .   .

Know'st thou not ghosts to sue?
    No love thou hast.
Else lie, as I will do,
    And breathe thy last.
So out of Life's fresh crown
Fall like a rose-leaf down.
    Thus are the ghosts to woo;
    Thus are all dreams made true,
        Ever to last!

THOMAS LOVELL BEDDOES

2. Gipsy Song

The faery beam upon you,
The stars to glister on you;
 A moon of light
 In the noon of night,
Till the fire-drake hath o'ergone you!
The wheel of fortune guide you,
The boy with the bow beside you;
 Run aye in the way
 Till the bird of day
And the luckier lot betide you!

BEN JONSON

3. By the Babe Unborn

If trees were tall and grasses short,
 As in some crazy tale,
And here and there a sea were blue
 Beyond the breaking pale,

If a fixed fire hung in the air
 To warm me one day through,
If deep green hair grew on great hills,
 I know what I should do.

In dark I lie: dreaming that there
 Are great eyes cold or kind,
And twisted streets and silent doors,
 And living men behind.

Let storm-clouds come: better an hour,
 And leave to weep and fight,
Than all the ages I have ruled
 The empires of the night.

I think that if they gave me leave
    Within that world to stand,
I would be good through all the day
    I spent in fairyland.

They should not hear a word from me
    Of selfishness or scorn,
If only I could find the door,
    If only I were born.

G. K. CHESTERTON

4. *The Seas*

When I awoke in the night I heard the trees sighing.
A gentle sound came into the room where I was lying,
And in the depths of a drowsy mind it seemed to me
That all the moonlit countryside was astir, like a sea,
With mile upon mile of sweet leaves tossing and crying
In time to the chime of another sea replying.

In the silence and sorrowing hush of the summer night,
While stars and a setting moon made a spirit-light,
I lay and listened an hour to the singing seas—
One song charmed from the garden limes and a breeze,
And the other coming up from that hidden sea
Whose waves break and fall in the depths of me.

STELLA GIBBONS

5. *Morning Dreams*

I asked of Night, that she would take me
    Where I could not go by day.
I asked of Day, he should not wake me
    Ere the sun was on his way;

For as the sun steals from the flowers
 The crystal dew by which they live,
He kills the memory of those hours
 Which Night, for my delight, will give.

6. Baffled

When the still fire burns like roses
 In the cavernous, empty night,
Through the small silent hours that watch
 From lamp light to dawn light,
We lie upstairs, a-sleeping deep,
 But in the house below
The puzzled tenants, blind and shy,
 Creep to and fro.
They are holding whispered conclave
 Together down there;
You may hear a sudden footfall
 Crack on a stair,
Or a window opened soft and quick,
 As if someone were
Seeking a clue to the strange house
 In the wide night air.

For they are baffled, strayed and lost,
 And the whispered things they say
Are puzzled echoes, murmured o'er,
 Of the words we said by day.
They touched the books that we laid down,
 With groping, blind-man hands,
As travellers who stray, sighing,
 Lost in strange lands.
They know not what the curious house
 Holds for their good or ill;
It is a maze without a clue,
 So dark, warm and still.

   • • • • •

And they are you and they are I;
    And while we lie sleeping,
Ourselves, bewildered by ourselves,
    Go blindly creeping
About the house we know by day,
    The things we love well,
Finding them fearful, far away,
    Incomprehensible.

.   .   .   .

We wake upstairs: the morning fills
    The still house with sun.
Away out of the clueless maze
    Soft feet run.

ROSE MACAULAY

V
DAYBREAK

1. From *The Salutation*

When silent I
  So many thousand, thousand years
Beneath the dust did in a chaos lie,
  How could I smiles or tears,
Or lips or hands or eyes or ears perceive?
Welcome ye treasures which I now receive.

I that so long
  Was nothing from eternity,
Did little think such joys as ear or tongue
  To celebrate or see:
Such sounds to hear, such hands to feel, such feet,
Beneath the skies on such a ground to meet.

New burnisht joys!
  Which yellow gold and pearls excel!
Such sacred treasures are the limbs in boys,
  In which a soul doth dwell;
Their organized joints and azure veins
More wealth include than all the world contains.

From dust I rise,
  And out of nothing now awake,
These brighter regions which salute mine eyes,
  A gift from God I take.
The earth, the seas, the light, the day, the skies,
The sun and stars are mine; if those I prize.

Long time before
  I in my mother's womb was born,
A God preparing did this glorious store,
  The world for me adorn.
Into this Eden so divine and fair,
So wide and bright, I come His son and heir.

A stranger here
Strange things doth meet, strange glories see;
Strange treasures lodg'd in this fair world appear,
Strange all and new to me;
But that they mine should be, who nothing was,
That strangest is of all, yet brought to pass.

THOMAS TRAHERNE

2. *The Night will Never Stay*

The night will never stay,
The night will still go by,
Though with a million stars
You pin it to the sky;
Though you bind it with the blowing wind
And buckle it with the moon,
The night will slip away
Like sorrow or a tune.

ELEANOR FARJEON

3. *Hunting-song of the Seeonee Pack*

As the dawn was breaking the Sambhur belled
Once, twice and again!
And a doe leaped up, and a doe leaped up
From the pond in the wood where the wild deer sup
This I, scouting alone, beheld,
Once, twice and again!

As the dawn was breaking the Sambhur belled
Once, twice and again!
And a wolf stole back, and a wolf stole back
To carry the word to the waiting pack,
And we sought and we found and we bayed on his track
Once, twice and again!

As the dawn was breaking the Wolf Pack yelled
    Once, twice and again!
Feet in the jungle that leave no mark!
Eyes that can see in the dark—the dark!
Tongue—give tongue to it! Hark! O hark!
    Once, twice and again!

RUDYARD KIPLING

4. Daybreak

After the dark of night
Spreads slowly up the glow
Into the starry height
Of daybreak piercing through.

Now gin the cocks to crow;
Runs lapwing, claw and crest;
From her green haunt the hare
Lopes wet with dew. The east

Gathers its cloudy host
Into its soundless pen;
Stirring in their warm sleep,
Beasts rise and graze again.

Now, with his face on fire,
And drenched with sunbeams through,
Sam, with his dappled team,
Drags out the iron plough.

Glistens with drops the grass;
Sighing, with joy, the trees
Stoop their green leafiness
Into the breeze.

Earth's wake now: every heart,
Wing, foot, and eye
Revels in light and heat:
The Sun's in the sky!

WALTER DE LA MARE

27

5. From *In Memoriam*

Till now the doubtful dusk reveal'd
>The knolls once more where, couch'd at ease,
>The white kine glimmer'd, and the trees
Laid their dark arms about the field:

And suck'd from out the distant gloom
>A breeze began to tremble o'er
>The large leaves of the sycamore,
And fluctuate all the still perfume,

And gathering freshlier overhead,
>Rock'd the full-foliaged elms, and swung
>The heavy-folded rose, and flung
The lilies to and fro, and said

'The dawn, the dawn,' and died away,
>And East and West, without a breath
>Mixt their dim lights, like life and death,
To broaden into boundless day.

ALFRED, LORD TENNYSON

6. From *Pippa Passes*

Day!
Faster and more fast,
O'er night's brim, day boils at last:
Boils, pure gold, o'er the cloud-cup's brim
Where spurting and suppressed it lay,
For not a froth-flake touched the rim
Of yonder gap in the solid gray
Of the eastern cloud, an hour away;
But forth one wavelet, then another, curled,
Till the whole sunrise, not to be suppressed,
Rose, reddened, and its seething breast
Flickered in bounds, grew gold, then overflowed the world. . . .

ROBERT BROWNING

7. *Early Light*

When morning is early, is early,
    the land lies cool
as the delicate floor
    of a limpid pool.

The spires of the churches rise
    from the still green meads,
like tapering fingers
    of water-weeds.

The farms in the fold of the hill,
    and the clear, carved trees,
have sunk to the bottom
    of crystal seas:

have sunk into seas of glass,
    and are drowned so deep
no ripple can shatter
    their shining sleep.

LILIAN BOWES LYON

VI
VERY EARLY

1. *Long Ago*

Birds in the world were waking;
Dawn was beyond the wood;
Youth at an open window
Tranced in the twilight stood;
Youth in springtime strangeness
Stilled in a mind-made past,
Seeing, beyond his limits,
Loveliness veiled and vast.

Youth, once mine, once wonder,
Ignorant, brimmed with tears,
Long have you wandered, laden
Head and heart with your years;
Yet in this moment's vision
Youth at the window stands,
Unforeboding, enchanted,
Holding the world in his hands.

SIEGFRIED SASSOON

2. From *Early Rising*

I arose early, O my true love!
I was awake and wide
To see the last star quenched above
And the moon lying on her side.

I saw the tops of the tall elms shine
Over the mist on the lea,
And the new bells upon the bine
Opened most silently;
And in the foggy dew the kine
Lay still as rocks in the sea.

31

The foggy dew lay on the flower
Silver and soft and chaste:
The turtle in her oaken tower
To waken made no haste:
Slept by her love another hour
And her two young embraced.

Mine was the solemn silence then,
And that clean tract of sky:
There was no smoke from hearths of men,
As yet no one went by:
The beast of night had sought his den,
The lark not climbed on high,

It was an hour of Eden; yea,
So still the time and slow,
I thought the sun mistook his way,
And was bewildered so
That coming he might bring a day
Lost since a thousand years ago:

A day of innocence and mirth,
A birds' day, day of prayer,
When every simple tongue of earth
A song or psalm might bear:
When love of God was something worth,
And holiness not killed with care.

RUTH PITTER

3. The Rivals

I heard a bird at dawn
Singing sweetly on a tree,
That the dew was on the lawn,
And the wind was on the lea;
But I didn't listen to him,
For he didn't sing to me!

I didn't listen to him,
For he didn't sing to me
That the dew was on the lawn,
And the wind was on the lea!
I was singing at the time,
Just as prettily as he!

I was singing all the time,
Just as prettily as he,
About the dew upon the lawn,
And the wind upon the lea!
So I didn't listen to him,
As he sang upon a tree!

JAMES STEPHENS

4. From *Vigils*

Down the glimmering staircase, past the pensive clock,
Childhood creeps on tiptoe, fumbles at the lock.
Out of night escaping, toward the arch of dawn,
What can childhood look for, over the wet lawn?

Standing in the strangeness of that garden air,
Ignorant adventure finds world wonder there:
Miles are more than distance when the cocks are crowing
And along the valley night's last goods-train going
Tells of earth untravelled and what lies beyond
Catching roach and gudgeon in the orchard pond.

SIEGFRIED SASSOON

5. *A Prayer in Spring*

Oh, give us pleasure in the flowers today;
And give us not to think so far away
As the uncertain harvest; keep us here
All simply in the springing of the year.

33   **D**

Oh, give us pleasure in the orchard white,
Like nothing else by day, like ghosts by night;
And make us happy in the happy bees,
The swarm dilating round the perfect trees.

And make us happy in the darting bird
That suddenly above the bees is heard,
The meteor that thrusts in with needle bill,
And off a blossom in mid air stands still.

For this is love and nothing else is love,
To which it is reserved for God above
To sanctify to what far ends He will,
But which it only needs that we fulfil.

ROBERT FROST

6. *Sonnet*

Rise up and do begin the day's adorning;
The Summer dark is but the dawn of day.
The last of sunset fades into the morning;
The morning calls you from the dark away.
The holy mist, the white mist of the morning
Was wreathing upward on my lonely way.
The way was waiting for your own adorning
That should complete the broad adornéd day.

Rise up and do begin the day's adorning;
The little eastern clouds are dapple grey:
There will be wind among the leaves today;
It is the very promise of the morning.
        Lux tua Via Mea: your light's my way—
        Then do rise up and make it perfect day.

HILAIRE BELLOC

7. *Reveille*

Wake: the silver dusk returning
    Up the beach of darkness brims,
And the ship of sunrise burning
    Strands upon the eastern rims.

Wake: the vaulted shadow shatters,
    Trampled to the floor it spanned,
And the tent of night in tatters
    Straws the sky-pavilioned land.

Up, lad, up, 'tis late for lying:
    Hear the drums of morning play;
Hark, the empty highways crying
    'Who'll beyond the hills away?'

Towns and countries woo together,
    Forelands beacon, belfries call;
Never lad that trod on leather
    Lived to feast his heart with all.

Up, lad: thews that lie and cumber
    Sunlit pallets never thrive;
Morns abed and daylight slumber
    Were not meant for men alive.

Clay lies still, but blood's a rover;
    Breath's a ware that will not keep.
Up, lad: when the journey's over
    There'll be time enough for sleep.

A. E. HOUSMAN

8. From *Corinna's Going a Maying*

Get up, get up for shame, the blooming morn
Upon her wings presents the god unshorn.
    See how Aurora throws her fair
    Fresh-quilted colours through the air:

Get up, sweet-slug-a-bed, and see
The dew-bespangling herb and tree.
Each flower has wept, and bow'd toward the East,
Above an hour since; yet you not drest,
    Nay! not so much as out of bed?
    When all the birds have Matins said,
    And sung their thankful hymns: 'tis sin,
    Nay, profanation to keep in,
When as a thousand virgins on this day,
Spring, sooner than the lark, to fetch in May.

    .   .   .   .   .   .

There's not a budding boy, or girl, this day,
But is got up, and gone to bring in May.
    A deal of Youth, ere this, is come
    Back, and with white-thorn laden home.
    Some have despatcht their cakes and cream,
    Before that we have left to dream:
And some have wept, and woo'd, and plighted troth,
And chose their priest, ere we can cast off sloth:
    Many a green-gown has been given:
    Many a kiss, both odd and even:
    Many a glance too has been sent
    From out the eye, love's firmament:
Many a jest told of the keys betraying
This night, and locks pickt, yet we're not a Maying.

Come, let us go, while we are in our prime;
And take the harmless folly of the time.
    We shall grow old apace, and die
    Before we know our liberty.
    Our life is short; and our days run
    As fast away as does the sun:
And as a vapour, or a drop of rain
Once lost, can ne'er be found again:
    So when or you or I are made
    A fable, song, or fleeting shade;

All love, all liking, all delight
Lies drown'd with us in endless night.
Then while time serves, and we are but decaying;
Come, my Corinna, come, let's go a Maying.

ROBERT HERRICK

9. Hazel Buds

Now breaks the sheath and spreads the leaf!
The bank beneath, the branch above,
Are set with nests, are homes of love.
So good-bye, grief!

With restful haste and gentle strife
Pink hazel stipules are unfurled,
Pink dawns are flung across the world.
So welcome, life!

MARY WEBB

10. A Morning Song

For the First Day of Spring

Morning has broken
Like the first morning,
Blackbird has spoken
    Like the first bird.
        Praise for the singing!
        Praise for the morning!
        Praise for them, springing
        From the First Word!

Sweet the rain's new fall
Sunlit from heaven,
Like the first dewfall
    On the first grass.

Praise for the sweetness
Of the wet garden,
Sprung in completeness
Where his feet pass.

Mine is the sunlight!
Mine is the morning
Born of the one light
Eden saw play!
Praise with elation,
Praise every morning,
God's re-creation
Of the new day!

ELEANOR FARJEON

VII
INVITATIONS

1. *Gellatley's Song to the Deerhounds*

Hie away, hie away,
Over bank and over brae,
Where the copsewood is the greenest,
Where the fountains glisten sheenest,
Where the lady-fern grows strongest,
Where the morning dew lies longest,
Where the black-cock sweetest sips it,
Where the fairy latest trips it:
Hie to haunts right seldom seen,
Lovely, lonesome, cool, and green,
Over bank and over brae,
Hie away, hie away.

SIR WALTER SCOTT

2. From *Come When the Leaf Comes*

Come when the leaf comes, angle with me,
Come when the bee hums over the lea,
    Come with the wild flowers—
    Come with the mild showers—
Come when the singing bird calleth for thee!

Then to the stream side gladly we'll hie,
Where the grey trout glide silently by,
    Or in some still place
    Over the hill face
Hurrying onward, drop the light fly.

THOMAS TOD STODDART

3. From *To His Coy Mistress*

Now therefore, while the youthful hue
Sits on thy skin like morning lew,[1]
And while thy willing soul transpires
At every pore with instant fires,

[1] Dew.

Now let us sport us while we may;
And now, like am'rous birds of prey,
Rather at once our time devour,
Than languish in his slow-chapt pow'r.
Let us roll all our strength, and all
Our sweetness, up into one ball:
And tear our pleasures with rough strife,
Through the iron gates of life;
Thus, though we cannot make our sun
Stand still, yet we will make him run.

ANDREW MARVELL

4. Song from *The Gentle Craft*

The primrose in the green forest,
   the violets they be gay:
The double daisies and the rest,
   that trimly decks the way,
Doth move the spirits with brave delights,
   whose beauties darlings be:
With hey tricksie, trim go tricksie,
   under the greenwood tree.

THOMAS DELONEY

5. From *To Jane: The Invitation*

Best and brightest, come away!
Fairer far than this fair Day,
Which, like thee to those in sorrow,
Comes to bid a sweet good-morrow
To the rough Year just awake
In its cradle on the brake.

.   .   .   .   .

Away, away, from men and towns,
To the wild wood and the downs—

To the silent wilderness
Where the soul need not repress
Its music, lest it should not find
An echo in another's mind,
While the touch of Nature's art
Harmonizes heart to heart.
I leave this notice on my door
For each accustomed visitor:—
'I am gone into the fields
To take what this sweet hour yields;—
Reflection, you may come tomorrow,
Sit by the fireside with Sorrow.—
You with the unpaid bill, Despair,—
You, tiresome verse-reciter, Care,—
I will pay you in the grave,—
Death will listen to your stave.
Expectation too, be off!
Today is for itself enough;
Hope, in pity mock not Woe
With smiles, nor follow where I go;
Long having lived on thy sweet food,
At length I find one moment's good
After long pain—with all your love,
This you never told me of.'

Radiant Sister of the Day,
Awake! arise! and come away!
To the wild woods and the plains,
And the pools where winter rains
Image all their roof of leaves,
Where the pine its garland weaves
Of sapless green and ivy dun
Round stems that never kiss the sun;
Where the lawns and pastures be,
And the sandhills of the sea;—
Where the melting hoar-frost wets
The daisy-star that never sets,
The wind-flowers, and the violets,

Which yet join not scent to hue,
Crown the pale year weak and new;
When the night is left behind
In the deep east, dun and blind,
And the blue noon is over us,
And the multitudinous
Billows murmur at our feet,
Where the earth and ocean meet,
And all things seem only one
In the universal sun.

PERCY BYSSHE SHELLEY

6. Mine Host

(From the Chinese)

Linger not in my library,
If you seek in it wisdom, not pleasure.
Before you turn to my bookshelves, listen.
Green ivy fingers tap the window,
Calling the eyes to the slope of orchard.
My son is fishing in the pond,
And beyond,
The grass is blanched as for a wedding,
Under the orchard trees, with idle blossom.
My library door adjoins the orchard—
An you wisely seek for pleasure,
It will let you pass.

ALUN LEWIS

7. From The Gardener

Over the green and yellow rice-fields sweep the shadows of the autumn clouds followed by the swift-chasing sun.

The bees forget to sip their honey; drunken with light they foolishly hover and hum.

The ducks in the islands of the river clamour in joy for mere nothing.

Let none go back home, brothers, this morning, let none go to work.

Let us take the blue sky by storm and plunder space as we run.

Laughter floats in the air like foam on the flood.

Brother, let us squander our morning in futile songs.

RABINDRANATH TAGORE

VIII
THE DAY'S PLAY

1. *A Boy's Song*

Where the pools are bright and deep,
Where the grey trout lies asleep,
Up the river and over the lea—
That's the way for Billy and me.

Where the blackbird sings the latest,
Where the hawthorn blooms the sweetest,
Where the nestlings chirp and flee,
That's the way for Billy and me.

Where the mowers mow the cleanest,
Where the hay lies thick and greenest;
There to trace the homeward bee,
That's the way for Billy and me.

Where the hazel bank is steepest,
Where the shadow falls the deepest,
Where the clustering nuts fall free,
That's the way for Billy and me.

Why the boys should drive away
Little sweet maidens from their play,
Or love to banter and fight so well,
That's the thing I never could tell.

But this I know, I love to play,
Through the meadow, among the hay;
Up the water and over the lea,
That's the way for Billy and me.

JAMES HOGG

2. *A Song*

With Love among the haycocks
We played at hide and seek;

He shut his eyes and counted—
   We hid among the hay—
Then he a haycock mounted,
   And spied us where we lay;

And O! the merry laughter
Across the hayfield after!

RALPH HODGSON

3. *The Shade-catchers*

I think they were about as high
As haycocks are. They went running by
Catching bits of shade in the sunny street:
'I've got one,' cried sister to brother.
      'I've got two.' 'Now I've got another.'
But scudding away on their little bare feet,
They left the shade in the sunny street.

CHARLOTTE MEW

4. *The Horse-trough*

Clouds of children round the trough
Splash and clatter in the sun:
Their clouted shoes are mostly off,
And some are quarrelling, and one
Cools half her face, nose downward bubbling,
Wetting her clothes and never troubling;
Bobble, bobble, bobble there
Till bubbles like young earthquakes heave
The orange islands of her hair,
And tidal waves run up her sleeve;
Another's tanned as brown as bistre;
Another ducks his little sister,

47

And all are mixed in such a crowd
And tell their separate joys so loud
That who can be this silent one,
This dimpled, pensive, baby one?
—She sits the sunny steps so still
For hours, trying hard to kill
One fly at least of those that buzz
So cannily. . . .

And then she does.

RICHARD HUGHES

5. To a Child Dancing in the Wind

Dance there upon the shore;
What need have you to care
For wind or water's roar?
And tumble out your hair
That the salt drops have wet;
Being young you have not known
The fool's triumph, nor yet
Love lost as well as won,
Nor the best labourer dead
And all the sheaves to bind.
What need have you to dread
The monstrous crying of the wind?

W. B. YEATS

6. Amphibian

The fancy I had today,
    Fancy which turned a fear!
I swam far out in the bay,
    Since waves laughed warm and clear.

I lay and looked at the sun,
 The noon-sun looked at me:
Between us two, no one
 Live creature, that I could see.

Yes! There came floating by
 Me, who lay floating too,
Such a strange butterfly!
 Creature as dear as new:

Because the membraned wings
 So wonderful, so wide,
So sun-suffused, were things
 Like soul and nought beside.

A handbreadth over head!
 All of the sea my own,
It owned the sky instead;
 Both of us were alone.

ROBERT BROWNING

7. *Angler's Song*

Man's life is but vain, for 'tis subject to pain
And sorrow, and short as a bubble;
'Tis a hodgepodge of business, and money, and care,
And care, and money, and trouble.

But we'll take no care when the weather proves fair;
Nor will we vex now though it rain;
We'll banish all sorrow, and sing till tomorrow
And angle and angle again.

Anon from *The Compleat Angler*

8. The Further Bank

I long to go over there to the further bank of the river,
Where those boats are tied to the bamboo poles in a line,
Where men cross over in their boats in the morning with ploughs on their shoulders to till far-away fields;
Where the cowherds make their lowing cattle swim across to the riverside pasture;
Whence they all come back home in the evening, leaving the jackals to howl in the island overgrown with weeds.
Mother, if you don't mind, I should like to become the boatman of the ferry when I am grown up.

They say there are strange pools hidden behind that high bank,
Where flocks of wild ducks come when the rains are over, and thick reeds grow round the margins where water-birds lay their eggs;
Where snipes with their dancing tails stamp their tiny footprints upon the clean soft mud;
Where in the evening the tall grasses crested with white flowers invite the moonbeam to float upon their waves.
Mother, if you don't mind, I should like to become the boatman of the ferryboat when I am grown up.

I shall cross and cross back from bank to bank, and all the boys and girls of the village will wonder at me while they are bathing.
When the sun climbs the mid sky and morning wears on to noon, I shall come running to you, saying, 'Mother, I am hungry!'
When the day is done and the shadows cower under the trees, I shall come back in the dusk.
I shall never go away from you into the town to work like father.
Mother, if you don't mind, I should like to become the boatman of the ferryboat when I am grown up.

RABINDRANATH TAGORE

50

IX
SOLITUDE

1. *The Hut*

Whatever place is poor and small,
The Hut was poorer still,
Stuck, like a snail upon a wall,
On what we called a hill.

It leaned upon an apple-tree
Whose laden branches lay
On the hot roof voluptuously,
And murmured all the day.

One hand-broad window, full of boughs,
Mirrored the flaming hearth
As if the Dryad warmed her house
With fire from under earth;

And one the livid lasting-pea
And staring marigold,
The knotty oak and elder-tree
Showed in the morning cold.

The sapling ash had mined the floor,
The chimney flew the bine;
The doorway was without a door,
But flaunted eglantine.

The swallow built about the beam,
The rat was much at home:
And there one foolish child would dream,
Where sorrow could not come.

RUTH PITTER

2. *The Cliff-top*

The cliff-top has a carpet
    Of lilac, gold and green:
The blue sky bounds the ocean
    The white clouds scud between.

A flock of gulls are wheeling
      And wailing round my seat;
Above my head the heaven,
      The sea beneath my feet.

ROBERT BRIDGES

3. From *The Land*

Far from shrewd companies,
Far from the flares,
Here where the summer is,
And laden airs,
Here where no voice of men
Down in the wood
Startles the water-hen
And small black brood,
Here where the branches wave
And day is green,
Making the wood a cave
Aquamarine,
Here where the insects hum,
And dragon-fly,
Here we clandestine come,
Marvell and I.

V. SACKVILLE-WEST

4. *The Goat Paths*

I

The crooked paths
Go every way
Upon the hill
—They wind about
Through the heather,
In and out
Of a quiet
Sunniness.

And the goats,
Day after day,
Stray
In sunny
Quietness;
Cropping here,
And cropping there
—As they pause,
And turn,
And pass—
Now a bit
Of heather spray,
Now a mouthful
Of the grass.

II

In the deeper
Sunniness;
In the place
Where nothing stirs;
Quietly
In quietness;
In the quiet
Of the furze
They stand a while;
They dream;
They lie;
They stare
Upon the roving sky.

If you approach
They run away!
They will stare,
And stamp,
And bound,
With a sudden angry sound,
To the sunny
Quietude;

To crouch again,
Where nothing stirs,
In the quiet
Of the furze:
To crouch them down again,
And brood,
In the sunny
Solitude.

III

Were I but
As free
As they,
I would stray
Away
And brood;
I would beat
A hidden way,
Through the quiet
Heather spray,
To a sunny
Solitude.

And should you come
I'd run away!
I would make an angry sound,
I would stare,
And stamp,
And bound
To the deeper
Quietude;
To the place
Where nothing stirs
In the quiet
Of the furze.

In that airy
Quietness
I would dream
As long as they:
Through the quiet
Sunniness
I would stray
Away
And brood,
All among
The heather spray,
In a sunny
Solitude.

—I would think
Until I found
Something
I can never find;
—Something
Lying
On the ground,
In the bottom
Of my mind.

JAMES STEPHENS

5. From *Solitude*

I love the stillness of the wood:
    I love the music of the rill:
I love to couch in pensive mood
    Upon some silent hill.

Scarce heard, beneath yon arching trees,
    The silver-crested ripples pass;
And, like a mimic brook, the breeze
    Whispers among the grass.

Here from the world I win release,
    Nor scorn of men, nor footstep rude,
Break in to mar the holy peace
    Of this great solitude.

.   .   .   .   .   .

Ye golden hours of Life's young spring,
    Of innocence, of love of truth!
Bright, beyond all imagining,
    Thou fairy-dream of youth!

I'd give all wealth that years have piled,
    The slow result of Life's decay,
To be once more a little child
    For one bright summer-day.

LEWIS CARROLL

MORNING GLORY

I

LONDON TOWN

1. *Sonnet Composed upon Westminster Bridge*

Earth has not anything to show more fair:
Dull would he be of soul who could pass by
A sight so touching in its majesty:
The City now doth, like a garment, wear
The beauty of the morning; silent, bare,
Ships, towers, domes, theatres, and temples lie
Open unto the fields, and to the sky;
All bright and glittering in the smokeless air.
Never did sun more beautifully steep
In his first splendour, valley, rock, or hill;
Ne'er saw I, never felt, a calm so deep!
The river glideth at his own sweet will:
Dear God! the very houses seem asleep;
And all that mighty heart is lying still!

WILLIAM WORDSWORTH

2. *The Shining Streets of London*

Now, in the twilight, after rain
The wet black street shines out again;
And, softening through the coloured gloom,
The lamps like burning tulips bloom.

Now, lighted shops, down aisles of mist,
Smoulder in gold and amethyst;
And paved with fragments of the skies
Our sooty town like Venice lies.

For, streaked with tints of cloud and moon,
The tides of a bewitched lagoon
Into the solid squares we know
And round the shadowy minster flow;

Till even that emperor of the street,
The bluff policeman on his beat,
Reflected there with portly pride
From boots to helmet, floats enskied.

Now every woman's face is fair,
And Cockney lovers walk on air,
And every road, in broken gleams,
Mirrors a travelling throng of dreams.

Like radiant galleons, lifting high
Their scutcheoned prows against the sky,
With lamps that near you, blazing white,
Or shine in crimson through the night,

Buses (with coloured panes that spill
A splash of cherry or daffodil)
And lighted faces, row on row,
From darkness into darkness go.

O Love, what need have you and I
Of vine and palm and azure sky,
And who would sail for Greece or Rome
When such a highway leads him home?

ALFRED NOYES

3. *A London Voluntary*

Scherzando

Down through the ancient Strand
The spirit of October, mild and boon
And sauntering, takes his way
This golden end of afternoon,
As though the corn stood yellow in all the land,
And the ripe apples dropped to the harvest-moon.

Lo! the round sun, half-down the western slope—
Seen as along an unglazed telescope—
Lingers and lolls, loth to be done with day:
Gifting the long, lean, lanky street
And its abounding confluences of being
With aspects generous and bland;

Making a thousand harnesses to shine
As with new ore from some enchanted mine,
And every horse's coat so full of sheen
He looks new tailored, and every bus feels clean,
And never a hansom but is worth the feeing;
And every jeweller within the pale
Offers a real Arabian Night for sale;
And even the roar
Of the strong streams of toil, that pause and pour
Eastward and westward, sounds suffused—
Seems as it were bemused
And blurred, and like the speech
Of lazy seas on a lotus-haunted beach—
With this enchanted lustrousness,
This mellow magic, that (as a man's caress
Brings back to some faded face, beloved before,
A heavenly shadow of the grace it wore
Ere the poor eyes were minded to beseech)
Old things transfigures, and you hail and bless
Their looks of long-lapsed loveliness once more:
Till Clement's, angular and cold and staid,
Gleams forth in glamour's very stuff arrayed;
And Bride's, her aëry, unsubstantial charm
Through flight on flight of springing, soaring stone
Grown flushed and warm,
Laughs into life full-mooded and fresh-blown;
And the high majesty of Paul's
Uplifts a voice of living light, and calls—
Calls to his millions to behold and see
How goodly this his London Town can be!

For earth and sky and air
Are golden everywhere,
And golden with a gold so suave and fine
The looking on it lifts the heart like wine.
Trafalgar Square
(The fountains volleying golden glaze)
Shines like an angel-market. High aloft

61

Over his couchant Lions, in a haze
Shimmering and bland and soft,
A dust of chrysoprase,
Our Sailor takes the golden gaze
Of the saluting sun, and flames superb,
As once he flamed it on his ocean round.
The dingy dreariness of the picture-place,
Turned very nearly bright,
Takes on a luminous transiency of grace,
And shows no more a scandal to the ground.
The very blind man pottering on the kerb,
Among the posies and the ostrich feathers
And the rude voices touched with all the weather
Of all the long, varying year,
Shares in the universal alms of light.
The windows, with their fleeting, flickering fires,
The height and spread of frontage shining sheer,
The quiring signs, the rejoicing roofs and spires—
'Tis El Dorado—El Dorado plain,
The Golden City! And when a girl goes by,
Look! as she turns her glancing head,
A call of gold is floated from her ear!
Golden, all golden! In a golden glory,
Long-lapsing down a golden coasted sky,
The day, not dies, but seems
Dispersed in wafts and drifts of gold, and shed
Upon a past of golden song and story
And memories of gold and golden dreams.

W. E. HENLEY

4. November Blue

O heavenly colour, London town
    Has blurred it from her skies;
And, hooded in an earthly brown,
    Unheaven'd the city lies.

No longer, standard-like, this hue
　　Above the broad road flies;
Nor does the narrow street the blue
　　Wear, slender pennon-wise.

But when the gold and silver lamps
　　Colour the London dew,
And, misted by the winter damps,
　　The shops shine bright anew—
Blue comes to earth, it walks the street,
　　It dyes the wide air through;
A mimic sky about their feet,
　　The throng go crowned with blue.

ALICE MEYNELL

5. *London Snow*

When men were all asleep the snow came flying,
In large white flakes falling on the city brown,
Stealthily and perpetually settling and loosely lying,
　　Hushing the latest traffic of the drowsy town;
Deadening, muffling, stifling its murmurs failing;
Lazily and incessantly floating down and down:
　　Silently sifting and veiling road, roof and railing;
Hiding difference, making unevenness even,
Into angles and crevices softly drifting and sailing.
　　All night it fell, and when full inches seven
It lay in the depth of its uncompacted lightness,
The clouds blew off from a high and frosty heaven;
　　And all woke earlier for the unaccustomed brightness
Of the winter dawning, the strange unheavenly glare:
The eye marvelled—marvelled at the dazzling whiteness;
　　The ear hearkened to the stillness of the solemn air;
No sound of wheel rumbling nor of foot falling,
And the busy morning cries came thin and spare.
　　Then boys I heard, as they went to school, calling,

They gathered up the crystal manna to freeze
Their tongues with tasting, their hands with snowballing;
　　Or rioted in a drift, plunging up to the knees;
Or peering up from under the white-mossed wonder,
'O look at the trees!' they cried, 'O look at the trees!'

　　With lessened load a few carts creak and blunder,
Following along the white deserted way,
A country company long dispersed asunder.

　　When now already the sun, in pale display
Standing by Paul's high dome, spread forth below
His sparkling beams, and awoke the stir of the day.

　　For now doors open, and war is waged with the snow;
And trains of sombre men, past tale of number,
Tread long brown paths, as toward their toil they go:

　　But even for them awhile no cares encumber
Their minds diverted; the daily word is unspoken,
The daily thoughts of labour and sorrow slumber
At the sight of the beauty that greets them, for the charm
　　they have broken.

ROBERT BRIDGES

II

OUT IN THE COUNTRY

1. From *Frost at Midnight*

        . . . I was reared
In the great city, pent 'mid cloisters dim,
And saw nought lovely but the sky and stars.
But *thou*, my babe! shalt wander like a breeze
By lakes and sandy shores, beneath the crags
Of ancient mountain, and beneath the clouds,
Which image in their bulk both lakes and shores
And mountain crags: so shalt thou see and hear
The lovely shapes and sounds intelligible
Of that eternal language, which thy God
Utters, who from eternity doth teach
Himself in all, and all things in himself.
Great universal Teacher! he shall mould
Thy spirit, and by giving make it ask.

Therefore all seasons shall be sweet to thee,
Whether the summer clothe the general earth
With greenness, or the redbreast sit and sing
Betwixt the tufts of snow on the bare branch
Of mossy apple-tree, while the nigh thatch
Smokes in the sun-thaw; whether the eave-drops fall
Heard only in the trances of the blast,
Or if the secret ministry of frost
Shall hang them up in silent icicles,
Quietly shining to the quiet Moon.

SAMUEL TAYLOR COLERIDGE

2. From *The Land* (*Winter*)

The country habit has me by the heart,
For he's bewitched forever who has seen,
Not with his eyes but with his vision, Spring
Flow down the woods and stipple leaves with sun,
As each man knows the life that fits him best,
The shape it makes in his soul, the tune, the tone,

And after ranging on a tentative flight
Stoops like the merlin to the constant lure.
The country habit has me by the heart.
I never hear the sheep-bells in the fold,
Nor see the ungainly heron rise and flap
Over the marsh, nor hear the asprous corn
Clash, as the reapers set the sheaves in shocks
(That like a tented army dream away
The night beneath the moon in silver fields),
Nor watch the stubborn team of horse and man
Graven upon the skyline, nor regain
The sign-posts on the roads towards my home
Bearing familiar names—without a strong
Leaping of recognition; only here
Lies peace after uneasy truancy;
Here meet and marry many harmonies,
—All harmonies being ultimately one,—
Small mirroring majestic; for as earth
Rolls on her journey, so her little fields
Ripen or sleep, and the necessities
Of seasons match the planetary law.
So truly stride between the earth and heaven
Sowers of grain: so truly in the spring
Earth's orbit swings both blood and sap to rhythm,
And infinite and humble are at one;
So the brown hedger, through the evening lanes
Homeward returning, sees above the ricks,
Sickle in hand, the sickle in the sky.

V. SACKVILLE-WEST

3. The Birthright

We who were born
In country places,
Far from cities
And shifting faces,

We have a birthright
No man can sell,
And a secret joy
No man can tell.

For we are kindred
To lordly things,
The wild duck's flight
And the white owl's wings;
To pike and salmon,
To bull and horse,
The curlew's cry
And the smell of gorse.

Pride of trees,
Swiftness of streams,
Magic of frost
Have shaped our dreams:
No baser vision
Their spirit fills
Who walk by right
On the naked hills.

EILUNED LEWIS

4. Sonnet

Lift up your hearts in Gumber, laugh the Weald
And you my mother the Valley of Arun sing.
Here am I homeward from my wandering,
Here am I homeward and my heart is healed.
You my companions whom the World has tired
Come out to greet me. I have found a face
More beautiful than Gardens; more desired
Than boys in exile love their native place.

Lift up your hearts in Gumber, laugh the Weald
And you most ancient Valley of Arun sing.
Here am I homeward from my wandering,
Here am I homeward and my heart is healed.
If I was thirsty, I have heard a spring.
If I was dusty, I have found a field.

HILAIRE BELLOC

5. Inversnaid

This darksome burn, horseback brown,
His rollrock highroad roaring down,
In coop and in comb the fleece of his foam
Flutes and low to the lake falls home.

A windpuff-bonnet of fawn-froth
Turns and twindles over the broth
Of a pool so pitchblack, fell-frowning,
It rounds and rounds Despair to drowning.

Degged with dew, dappled with dew
Are the groins of the braes that the brook treads through,
Wiry heathpacks, flitches of fern,
And the beadbonny ash that sits over the burn.

What would the world be, once bereft
Of wet and wildness? Let them be left,
O let them be left, wildness and wet;
Long live the weeds and the wilderness yet.

GERARD MANLEY HOPKINS

6. Wiltshire Downs

The cuckoo's double note
Loosened like bubbles from a drowning throat
Floats through the air
In mockery of pipit, lark and stare.

The stable-boys thud by
Their horses slinging divots at the sky
And with bright hooves
Printing the sodden turf with lucky grooves.

As still as windhover
A shepherd in his flapping coat leans over
His tall sheep-crook
And shearlings, tegs and yoes cons like a book.

And one tree-crowned long barrow
Stretched like a sow that has brought forth her farrow
Hides a king's bones
Lying like broken sticks among the stones.

ANDREW YOUNG

7. *Real Property*

Tell me about that harvest field.
Oh! Fifty acres of living bread.
The colour has painted itself on my heart.
The form is patterned in my head.

So now I take it everywhere;
See it whenever I look round;
Hear it growing through every sound,
Know exactly the sound it makes—
Remembering, as one must all day,
Under the pavement the live earth aches.

Trees are at the farther end,
Limes all full of the mumbling bee:
So there must be a harvest field
Whenever one thinks of a linden tree.

A hedge is about it, very tall,
Hazy and cool, and breathing sweet.
Round paradise is such a wall
And all the day, in such a way,
In paradise the wild birds call.

You only need to close your eyes
And go within your secret mind,
And you'll be into paradise:
I've learnt quite easily to find
Some linden trees and drowsy bees,
A tall sweet hedge with the corn behind.

I will not have that harvest mown:
I'll keep the corn and leave the bread.
I've bought that field; it 's now my own:
I've fifty acres in my head.
I take it as a dream to bed.
I carry it about all day. . . .

Sometimes when I have found a friend
I give a blade of corn away.

HAROLD MONRO

8. On Yes Tor

Beneath our feet, the shuddering bogs
    Made earthquakes of their own,
For greenish-grizzled furtive frogs
    And lizards lithe and brown;

And high to east and south and west,
    Girt round with feet of gorse,
Lay, summering, breast by giant breast,
    The titan brood of tors;

Golden and phantom-pale they lay,
    Calm in the cloudless light,
Like gods that, slumbering, still survey
    The obsequious infinite.

Plod, plod, through herbage thin or dense,
    Past chattering rills of quartz;
Across brown bramble-coverts, whence
    The shy black ouzel darts;

Through empty leagues of broad, bare lands
    Beneath the empty skies,
Clutched in the grip of those vast hands,
    Cowed by those golden eyes,

We fled beneath their scornful stare,
    Like terror-hunted dogs,
More timid than the lizards were,
    And shyer than the frogs.

EDMUND GOSSE

III

THE SEA! THE SEA!

1. *The Sea Gipsy*

I am fevered with the sunset,
I am fretful with the bay,
For the wander-thirst is on me
And my soul is in Cathay.

There's a schooner in the offing,
With her topsails shot with fire,
And my heart has gone aboard her
For the Islands of Desire.

I must forth again tomorrow!
With the sunset I must be
Hull down on the trail of rapture
In the wonder of the sea.

RICHARD HOVEY

2. *A Wanderer's Song*

A wind's in the heart of me, a fire's in my heels,
I am tired of brick and stone and rumbling wagon-wheels;
I hunger for the sea's edge, the limits of the land,
Where the wild old Atlantic is shouting on the sand.

Oh I'll be going, leaving the noises of the street,
To where a lifting foresail-foot is yanking at the sheet;
To a windy, tossing anchorage where yawls and ketches ride,
Oh I'll be going, going, until I meet the tide.

And first I'll hear the sea-wind, the mewing of the gulls,
And clucking, sucking of the sea about the rusty hulls,
The songs at the capstan in the hooker warping out,
And then the heart of me'll know I'm there or thereabout.

Oh I am tired of brick and stone, the heart of me is sick,
For windy green, unquiet sea, the realm of Moby Dick;
And I'll be going, going, from the roaring of the wheels,
For a wind's in the heart of me, a fire's in my heels.

JOHN MASEFIELD

3. *East Anglian Bathe*

Oh when the early morning at the seaside
 Took us with hurrying steps from Horsey Mere
To see the whistling bent-grass on the leeside
 And then the tumbled breaker-line appear,
On high, the clouds with mighty adumbration
 Sailed over us to seaward fast and clear
And jellyfish in quivering isolation
 Lay silted in the dry sand of the breeze
And we, along the table-land of beach blown
 Went gooseflesh from our shoulders to our knees
And ran to catch the football, each to each thrown,
 In the soft and swirling music of the seas.

There splashed about our ankles as we waded
 Those intersecting wavelets morning-cold,
And sudden dark a patch of sea was shaded,
 And sudden light another patch would hold
The warmth of whirling atoms in a sun-shot
 And underwater sandstorm green and gold.
So in we dived and louder than a gunshot
 Sea-water broke in fountains down the ear.
How cold the swim, how chattering cold the drying,
 How welcoming the inland reeds appear,
The wood-smoke and the breakfast and the frying,
 And your warm freshwater ripples, Horsey Mere.

JOHN BETJEMAN

4. *An Old Song Re-sung*

I saw a ship a-sailing, a-sailing, a-sailing,
With emeralds and rubies and sapphires in her hold;
And a bosun in a blue coat bawling at the railing,
Piping through a silver call that had a chain of gold;
The summer wind was failing and the tall ship rolled.

I saw a ship a-steering, a-steering, a-steering,
With roses in red thread worked upon her sails;
With sacks of purple amethysts, the spoils of buccaneering,
Skins of musky yellow wine, and silks in bales,
His merry men were cheering, hauling on the brails.

I saw a ship a-sinking, a-sinking, a-sinking,
With glittering sea-water splashing on her decks,
With seamen in her spirit-room singing songs and drinking,
Pulling claret bottles down, and knocking off the necks,
The broken glass was chinking as she sank among the wrecks.

JOHN MASEFIELD

5. *In a Boat*

Lady! Lady!
Upon Heaven-height,
Above the harsh morning
In the mere light.

Above the spindthrift
And above the snow,
Where no seas tumble,
And no winds blow.

The twisting tides,
And the perilous sands
Upon all sides
Are in your holy hands.

The wind harries
And the cold kills;
But I see your chapel
Over far hills.

My body is frozen,
My soul is afraid:
Stretch out your hands to me,
Mother and maid.

Mother of Christ,
And Mother of me,
Save me alive
From the howl of the sea.

If you will Mother me
Till I grow old,
I will hang in your chapel
A ship of pure gold.

HILAIRE BELLOC

6. *The Shell*

I

And then I pressed the shell
Close to my ear,
And listened well.

And straightway, like a bell,
Came low and clear
The slow, sad, murmur of far distant seas

Whipped by an icy breeze
Upon a shore
Wind-swept and desolate.

It was a sunless strand that never bore
The footprint of a man,
Nor felt the weight

Since time began
Of any human quality or stir,
Save what the dreary winds and waves incur.

II

And in the hush of waters was the sound
Of pebbles, rolling round;
For ever rolling, with a hollow sound:

And bubbling sea-weeds, as the waters go,
Swish to and fro
Their long cold tentacles of slimy grey:

There was no day;
Nor ever came a night
Setting the stars alight

No wonder at the moon:
Was twilight only, and the frightened croon,
Smitten to whimpers, of the dreary wind

And waves that journeyed blind . . .
And then I loosed my ear—Oh, it was sweet
To hear a cart go jolting down the street.

JAMES STEPHENS

7. *The Shell*

What has the sea swept up?
A Viking car, long mouldered in the peace
Of grey oblivion? Some dim-burning bowl
Of unmixed gold, from far-off island feasts?
Ropes of old pearls? Masses of ambergris?
Something of elfdom from the ghastly isles
Where white-hot rocks piece through the flying spindrift?
Or a pale sea-queen, close wound in a net of spells?

Nothing of these. Nothing of antique splendours
That have a weariness about their names:
But—fresh and new, in frail transparency,
Pink as a baby's nail, silky and veined
As a flower petal—this casket of the sea,
One shell.

MARY WEBB

8. From *Ecstasy*

I saw a frieze on whitest marble drawn
Of boys who sought for shells along the shore
Their white feet shedding pallor in the sea,
The shallow sea, the spring-time sea of green
That faintly creamed against the cold, smooth pebbles.

. . . .

One held a shell unto his shell-like ear
And there was music carven in his face,
His eyes half-closed, his lips just breaking open
To catch the lulling, mazy, coralline roar
Of numberless caverns filled with singing seas.

And all of them were hearkening as to singing
Of far-off voices thin and delicate,
Voices too fine for any mortal wind
To blow into the whorls of mortal ears—
And yet those sounds flowed from their grave, sweet faces.

And as I looked I heard the delicate music,
And I became as grave, as calm, as still
As those carved boys. I stood upon that shore,
I felt the cool sea dream around my feet,
My eyes were staring at the far horizon. . . .

W. J. TURNER

IV
FLOWERS AND TREES

1. The Apple Tree

Let there be Light!
In pink and white
The apple tree blooms for our delight.
In pink and white,
Its shout unheard,
The Logos itself, the Creative Word,
Burst from nothing; and all is stirred.
It blooms and blows and shrivels to fall
Down on the earth in a pink-white pall,
Withered? But look at each little green ball,
Crowned like a globe in the hand of God,
Each little globe on a shortening rod;
Soon to be rosy and well bestowed,
A cosmos now where the blossoms glowed
Constellated around the tree,
A cone that lifts to infinity.
Each rosy globe is as red as Mars;
And all the tree is a branch of stars.
What can we say but, 'Glory be!'
When God breaks out in an apple tree?

OLIVER ST JOHN GOGARTY

2. Narcissus Fields

The fields are in flower in the West,
The great narcissus fields.
The green grass-wave has a foaming crest,
And the breath of Cornwall yields
A tide of scent that flows
Over the seaweed smell;
'Twixt island and mainland it blows,
Sea-salt and asphodel:

As when, so long ago,
Olaf the Viking rover
Sailed to an isle he did not know,
And the flower breathed like a lover,
Wooing the pagan king
To light on Columba's shore.
The pagan came from the Cornish spring
Christian for evermore.

For the gentleness of the flower
Overwhelms the ocean-crest,
And Christ still walks on the wave this hour
When the fields breathe in the West.

ELEANOR FARJEON

3. *Loveliest of Trees*

Loveliest of trees, the cherry now
Is hung with bloom along the bough,
And stands about the woodland ride
Wearing white for Eastertide.

Now, of my threescore years and ten,
Twenty will not come again,
And take from seventy springs a score,
It only leaves me fifty more.

And since to look at things in bloom
Fifty springs are little room,
About the woodlands I will go
To see the cherry hung with snow.

A. E. HOUSMAN

4. Bounty

The full woods overflow
    Among the meadow's gold!
A blue-bell wave has rolled,
    Where crowded cowslips grow.
The drifting hawthorn snow
    Brims over hill and wold.
The full woods overflow
    Among the meadow's gold;
The ditches are aglow!
    The marshes cannot hold
Their kingcups manifold.
    Heav'n's beauty crowds below,
The full woods overflow!

MARY WEBB

5. From *To the Small Celandine*

Pansies, lilies, kingcups, daisies,
Let them live upon their praises;
Long as there's a sun that sets,
Primroses will have their glory;
Long as there are violets,
They will have a place in story:
There's a flower that shall be mine,
'Tis the little celandine.

Eyes of some men travel far
For the finding of a star;
Up and down the heavens they go,
Men that keep a mighty rout!
I'm as great as they, I trow,
Since the day I found thee out,
Little flower—I'll make a stir,
Like a sage astronomer.

.   .   .   .

Poets, vain men in their mood!
Travel with the multitude:
Never heed them; I aver
That they all are wanton wooers;
But the thrifty cottager,
Who stirs little out of doors,
Joys to spy thee near her home;
Spring is coming, thou art come!

WILLIAM WORDSWORTH

6. The Dandelion

I am the sun's remembrancer, the boy
Who runs in hedgerow, and in field and garden,
Showing his badge, a round-faced golden joy
With tips of flame. I bear my master's pardon
For my long, greedy roots. I bring his message
And pay his sovereign coin for my passage.
If any call me robber of the soil,
Let him but wait on windy weather, note
How easily, without a mortal's toil,
I change my gold to silver treasure, float
The fairy mintage on the air, and then
Defy the curse of all industrious men.

RICHARD CHURCH

7. A Spike of Green

When I went out
The sun was hot
It shone upon
My flower pot.

And there I saw
A spike of green
That no one else
Had ever seen!

On other days
The things I see
Are mostly old
Except for me.

But this green spike
So new and small
Had never yet
Been seen at all!

BARBARA BAKER

8. *Child's Song*

I have a garden of my own,
    Shining with flow'rs of ev'ry hue;
I lov'd it dearly while alone,
    But I shall love it more with you:
And there the golden bees shall come,
    In summer-time at break of morn,
And wake us with their busy hum,
    Around the Siha's fragrant thorn.

I have a fawn from Aden's land,
    On leafy buds and berries nurst;
And you shall feed him from your hand,
    Though he may start with fear at first.
And I will lead you where he lies
    For shelter in the noontide heat;
And you may touch his sleeping eyes,
    And feel his little silv'ry feet.

THOMAS MOORE

V

THE SWEET SPRING

1. *Eager Spring*

     Whirl, snow, on the blackbird's chatter;
You will not hinder his song to come.
East wind, Sleepless, you cannot scatter
Quince-bud, almond-bud,
Little grape-hyacinth's
Clustering brood,
Nor unfurl the tips of the plum.
No half-born stalk of lily stops;
There is sap in the storm-torn bush;
And, ruffled by gusts in a snowblurred copse,
'Pity to wait' sings a thrush.

Love, there are few Springs left for us;
They go, and the count of them as they go
Makes surer the count that is left for us.
More than the East wind, more than the snow,
I would put back these hours that bring
Buds and bees and are lost;
I would hold the night and the frost,
To save for us one more Spring.

                         GORDON BOTTOMLEY

2. From *In Memoriam*

Now fades the last long streak of snow,
       Now burgeons every maze of quick
       About the flowering squares, and thick
By ashen roots the violets blow.

Now rings the woodland loud and long,
       The distance takes a lovelier hue,
       And drown'd in yonder living blue
The lark becomes a sightless song.

Now dance the lights on lawn and lea,
       The flocks are whiter down the vale,
       And milkier every milky sail
On winding stream or distant sea;

Where now the seamew pipes, or dives
       In yonder greening gleam, and fly
       The happy birds, that change their sky
To build and brood; that live their lives

From land to land; and in my breast
       Spring wakes too; and my regret
       Becomes an April violet,
And buds and blossoms like the rest.

ALFRED, LORD TENNYSON

3. From *Diffugere Nives*, *1917* (*To J. C. S.*)

The snows have fled, the hail, the lashing rain,
       Before the spring.
The grass is starred with buttercups again,
       The blackbirds sing.

Now spreads the month that feast of lovely things
       We loved of old.
Once more the swallow glides with darkling wings
       Against the gold.

Now the brown bees about the peach trees boom
       Upon the walls;
And far away beyond the orchard's bloom
       The cuckoo calls.

MAURICE BARING

4. From *Spring*

The Spring comes linking and jinking through the woods,
Opening wi' gentle hand the bonnie green and yellow buds . . .

WILLIAM MILLER

5. Spring

Nothing is so beautiful as spring—
    When weeds, in wheels, shoot long and lovely and lush;
    Thrush's eggs look little low heavens, and thrush
Through the echoing timber does so rinse and wring
The ear, it strikes like lightnings to hear him sing;
    The glassy peartree leaves and blooms, they brush
    The descending blue; that blue is all in a rush
With richness; the racing lambs too have fair their fling.

What is all this juice and all this joy?
    A strain of the earth's sweet being in the beginning
In Eden garden.—Have, get, before it cloy,
    Before it cloud, Christ, lord, and sour with sinning,
Innocent mind and Mayday in girl and boy,
    Most, O maid's child, thy choice and worthy the winning.

GERARD MANLEY HOPKINS

6. Written in March

The cock is crowing,
The stream is flowing,
The small birds twitter,
The lake doth glitter,
    The green field sleeps in the sun;
The oldest and youngest
Are at work with the strongest;
The cattle are grazing,
Their heads never raising;
    There are forty feeding like one!

Like an army defeated
The snow hath retreated,
And now doth fare ill
On the top of the bare hill;

The ploughboy is whooping—anon—anon:
There's joy in the mountains;
There's life in the fountains;
Small clouds are sailing,
Blue sky prevailing;
The rain is over and gone!

WILLIAM WORDSWORTH

7. *The Lent Lily*

'Tis spring; come out to ramble
The hilly brakes around,
For under thorn and bramble
About the hollow ground
The primroses are found.

And there's the windflower chilly
With all the winds at play,
And there's the Lenten lily
That has not long to stay
And dies on Easter day.

And since till girls go maying
You find the primrose still,
And find the windflower playing
With every wind at will,
But not the daffodil,

Bring baskets now, and sally
Upon the spring's array,
And bear from hill and valley
The daffodil away
That dies on Easter day.

A. E. HOUSMAN

VI

SUMMERTIME

1. *Summer*

Winter is cold-hearted,
Spring is yea and nay,
Autumn is a weathercock
    Blown every way:
Summer days for me
When every leaf is on its tree;

When Robin's not a beggar,
And Jenny Wren's a bride,
And larks hang singing, singing, singing,
    Over the wheat-fields wide,
    And anchored lilies ride,
    And the pendulum spider
    Swings from side to side;

And blue-black beetles transact business,
    And gnats fly in a host,
And furry caterpillars hasten
    That no time be lost,
    And moths grow fat and thrive,
    And ladybirds arrive.

Before green apples blush,
Before green nuts embrown,
Why one day in the country
Is worth a month in town;
Is worth a day and a year
Of the dusty, musty, lag-last fashion
    That days drone elsewhere.

CHRISTINA ROSSETTI

2. *Song for a May Morning*

It is May, it is May!
And all earth is gay,
For at last old winter is quite away:

He lingered awhile on his cloak of snow,
To see the delicate primrose blow;
He saw it, and made no longer stay—
And now it is May, it is May!

It is May, it is May!
And we bless the day
When we first delightedly so can say;
April had beams amidst her showers;
Yet bare were her gardens, and cold her bowers;
And her frown would blight, and her smile betray,
But now it is May, it is May!

It is May, it is May!
And the slenderest spray
Holds up a few leaves to the ripening ray;
And the birds sing fearlessly out on high,
And there's not a cloud in the calm blue sky;
And the villagers join their roundelay—
For, oh! it is May, it is May!

It is May, it is May!
And the flowers obey
The beams which alone are more bright than they;
Yet they spring at the touch of the sun,
And opening their sweet eyes, one by one,
In a language of beauty seem all to say
And of perfume,—'tis May, it is May!

It is May, it is May!
And delights that lay
Chilled and enchained beneath winter sway,
Break forth again o'er the kindling soul,
And soften, and soothe it and bless it whole.
Oh! thoughts more tender than words can convey
Sigh out—It is May, it is May!

HERBERT TREVELYAN

3. From *Lady Clare*

It was the time when lilies blow,
    And clouds are highest up in air,
Lord Ronald brought a lily-white doe
    To give his cousin, Lady Clare.

ALFRED, LORD TENNYSON

4. *Summer Song*

At the time when blossoms fall from the cherry-tree,
On a day when orioles flitted from bough to bough,
You said you must stop, because your horse was tired;
I said I must go, because my silkworms were hungry.

WU TI
Translated by ARTHUR WALEY

5. *Look, Stranger*

Look, stranger, at this island now
The leaping light for your delight discovers,
Stand stable here
And silent be,
That through the channels of the ear
May wander like a river
The swaying sound of the sea.

Here at the small field's ending pause
Where the chalk wall falls to the foam, and its tall ledges
Oppose the pluck
And knock of the tide,
And the shingle scrambles after the suck-
ing surf, and the gull lodges
A moment on its sheer side.

Far off like floating seeds the ships
Diverge on urgent voluntary errands;
And the full view
Indeed may enter
And move in memory as now these clouds do,
That pass the harbour mirror
And all the summer through the water saunter.

W. H. AUDEN

6. Summer Song

There are white moon daisies in the mist of the meadow
    Where the flowered grass scatters its seeds like spray,
There are purple orchis by the wood-ways' shadow,
    There are pale dog-roses by the white highway;
    And the grass, the grass is tall, the grass is up for hay,
With daisies white like silver and the buttercups like gold,
    And it's oh! for once to play thro' the long, the lovely day,
To laugh before the year grows old!

There is silver moonlight on the breast of the river
    Where the willows tremble to the kiss of night,
Where the nine tall aspens in the meadow shiver,
    Shiver in the night wind that turns them white.
    And the lamps, the lamps are lit, the lamps the glow-
        worms light,
Between the silver aspens and the west's last gold.
    And it's oh! to drink delight in the lovely lonely night,
To be young before the heart grows old!

E. NESBIT

7. Trebetherick

We used to picnic where the thrift
    Grew deep and tufted to the edge;
We saw the yellow foam-flakes drift
    In trembling sponges on the ledge
Below us, till the wind would lift
    Them up the cliff and o'er the hedge.

Sand in the sandwiches, wasps in the tea,
Sun on our bathing dresses heavy with the wet,
Squelch on the bladder-wrack waiting for the sea,
Fleas round the tamarisk, an early cigarette.

From where the coastguard houses stood
    One used to see, below the hill,
The lichened branches of a wood
    In summer silver-cool and still;
And there the Shade of Evil could
    Stretch out at us from Shilla Mill.
            Thick with sloe and blackberry, uneven in the light,
            Lonely ran the hedge, the heavy meadow was remote,
            The oldest part of Cornwall was the wood as black as
                night,
            And the pheasant and the rabbit lay torn open at the
                throat.

But when a storm was at its height,
    And feathery slate was black in rain,
And tamarisks were hung with light
    And golden sand was brown again,
Spring tide and blizzard would unite
    And sea came flooding up the lane.
            Waves full of treasure then were roaring up the beach,
            Ropes round our mackintoshes, waders warm and
                dry,
            We waited for the wreckage to come swirling into
                reach,
            Ralph, Vasey, Alastair, Biddy, John, and I.

Then roller into roller curled
    And thundered down the rocky bay,
And we were in a water-world
    Of rain and blizzard, sea and spray,
And one against the other hurled
    We struggled round to Greenaway.

Blessèd be St Enodoc, blessèd be the wave,
Blessèd be the springy turf, we pray, pray to thee,
Give to our children all the happy days you gave
To Ralph, Vasey, Alastair, Biddy, John and me.

JOHN BETJEMAN

8. A Field in June

Greed is dumb at sight of so much gold
As these immaculate cups lightly hold,
Nor do we finger with fever'd covetous look
The smooth meandering silver of the brook.
Untaxable bounties entering the mind's eye
From deep meadow and diamond-dropping sky,
Wool-gathering clouds and contemplating trees
Casting palpable shade, those and these
Spell silence, till a skylark, newly risen,
Lets joy and desire out of the dark prison.

GERALD BULLETT

VII
FALL

1. October's Song

The forest's afire!
The forest's afire!
The maple is burning,
The sycamore's turning,
  The beech is alight!
Make a pyre! make a pyre!
Bring the oak to the fire!
The forest is glowing!
The greenleaf is flowing
  In flame out of sight!

ELEANOR FARJEON

2. Beech Leaves

In autumn down the beechwood path
The leaves lie thick upon the ground.
It's there I love to kick my way
And hear the crisp and crashing sound.

I am a giant, and my steps
Echo and thunder to the sky.
How the small creatures of the woods
Must quake and cower as I pass by!

This brave and merry noise I make
In summer also when I stride
Down to the shining, pebbly sea
And kick the frothing waves aside.

JAMES REEVES

3. October Boy

If you can catch a leaf, so they say
As it falls from the tree,
      Glad will you be,
For a year and a day.

99

But I say let the leaves lie on the ground.
  I will find my delight
          Galloping right
  Into this rustling mound.

Let others snatch happiness from the trees
  I will jump in this deep
          Mouldering heap
  Up to my knobbly knees.

VIRGINIA GRAHAM

4. October

  Mellow October,
He turns our green to yellow,
    Our drunk to sober,
Our shrill to bass and cello.

  Scatters our leaves,
Tears to wistful tatters,
    Or ties in sheaves,
All (so we think) that matters,

  Midsummer glory
Bared in her lusty humour
    To frost and fury,
With Winter the next comer.

  Rages October:
Yet in his moody pages,
    Scan we them over,
Sums up the golden ages.

  Glummer no story
Than his: yet every comma,
    Dropt seed of glory,
Betokens a new summer.

GERALD BULLETT

5. October

O hushed October morning mild,
Thy leaves have ripened to the fall;
Tomorrow's wind, if it be wild,
Should waste them all.
The crows above the forest call;
Tomorrow they may form and go.
O hushed October morning mild,
Begin the hours of this day slow.
Make the day seem to us less brief.
Hearts not averse to being beguiled,
Beguile us in the way you know.
Release one leaf at break of day;
At noon release another leaf;
One from our trees, one far away.
Retard the sun with gentle mist;
Enchant the land with amethyst.
Slow, slow!
For the grapes' sake, if they were all,
Whose leaves already are burnt with frost,
Whose clustered fruit must else be lost—
For the grapes' sake along the wall.

ROBERT FROST

6. Hot Cake

Winter has come; fierce is the cold;
In the sharp morning air new-risen we meet.
Rheum freezes in the nose;
Frost hangs about the chin.
For hollow bellies, for chattering teeth
    and shivering knees
What better than hot cake?
Soft as the down of spring,
Whiter than autumn floss!

Dense and swift the steam
Rises, swells, and spreads.
Fragrance flies through the air,
Is scattered far and wide,
Steals down along the wind and wets
The covetous mouth of passer-by.
Servants and grooms
Cast sidelong glances, munch the empty air.
They lick their lips who serve;
While lines of envious lackeys by the wall
Stand dryly swallowing.

SHU HUI (A.D. 265–306)
Translated by ARTHUR WALEY

7. *Winter the Huntsman*

Through his iron glades
Rides Winter the Huntsman.
All colour fades
As his horn is heard sighing.

For through the forest
His wild hooves crash and thunder
Till many a mighty branch
Is torn asunder.

And the red reynard creeps
To his hole near the river,
The copper leaves fall
And the bare trees shiver.

As night creeps from the ground,
Hides each tree from its brother,
And each dying sound
Reveals yet another.

Is it Winter the Huntsman
Who gallops through his iron glades,
Cracking his cruel whip
To the gathering shades?

OSBERT SITWELL

8. *Ice on the Round Pond*

This was a dog's day, when the land
Lay black and white as a Dalmatian
And kite chased terrier kite
In a Kerry Blue sky.

This was a boy's day, when the wind
Cut tracks in the sky on skates
And noon leaned over like a snowman
To melt in the sun.

This was a poet's day, when the mind
Lay paper-white in a winter's peace
And watched the printed bird-tracks
Turn into words.

PAUL DEHN

VIII

THE SINGING WIND

1. *Wind's Work*

Kate rose up early as fresh as a lark,
Almost in time to see vanish the dark;
Jack rather later, bouncing from bed,
Saw fade on the dawn's cheek the last flush of red:
Yet who knows
When the wind rose?

Kate went to watch the new lambs at their play
And stroke the white calf born yesterday;
Jack sought the wood where trees grow tall
As who would learn to swarm them all:
Yet who knows
Where the wind goes?

Kate has sown candy-tuft, lupins and peas,
Carnations, forget-me-not and heart's-ease;
Jack has sown cherry-pie, marigold,
Love-that-lies-bleeding and snap-dragons bold:
But who knows
What the wind sows?

Kate knows a thing or two useful at home,
Darns like a fairy, and churns like a gnome;
Jack is a wise man at shaping a stick,
Once he's in the saddle the pony may kick.
But hark to the wind how it blows!
None comes, none goes,
None reaps or mows,
No friends turn foes,
No hedge bears sloes,
And no cock crows,
But the wind knows!

T. STURGE MOORE

2. Listen!

Listen! the wind is rising,
and the air is wild with leaves;
we have had our summer evenings;
now for October eves!

The great beech trees lean forward,
and strip like a diver. We
had better turn to the fire
and shut our minds to the sea,

where the ships of youth are running
close-hauled on the edge of the wind,
with all adventure before them,
and only the old behind.

HUMBERT WOLFE

3. From *Stormy Day*

O look how the loops and balloons of bloom
Bobbing on long strings from the finger-ends
And knuckles of the lurching cherry-tree
Heap and hug, elbow and part, this wild day,
Like a careless carillon cavorting;
And the beaded whips of the beeches splay
And dip like anchored weed round a drowned rock,
And hovering effortlessly the rooks
Hang on the wind's effrontery as if
On hooks, then loose their hold and slide away
Like sleet sidewards down the warm swimming sweep
Of wind. O it is a lovely time when
Out of the sunk and rigid sumps of thought
Our hearts rise and race with new sounds and sights
And signs, tingling delightedly at the sting
And crunch of springless carts on gritty roads,

The caught kite dangling in the skinny wires,
The swipe of swallow across the eyes,
Striped awnings stretched on lawns. New things surprise
And stop us everywhere. . . .

W. R. RODGERS

4. *The Wind*

Blow colder, wind, and drive
My blood from hands and face nearer the heart.
Cry over ridges and down tapering coombs,
Carry the flying dapple of the clouds
Over the grass, over the soft-grained plough,
Stroke with your violent hands the hill's rough hair
    Against its usual set.
Snatch at the reins in my dead hands and push me
Out of the saddle, blow my labouring pony
Across the track. You only drive my blood
Nearer the heart from face and hands and plant it there,
Slowly burning, unseen, but alive and wonderful,
    A numb, confusèd joy!
This little world's in tumult. Far away
The dim waves rise and wrestle with each other
And fall down headlong on the beach. And here
Quick gusts fly up the funnels of the valleys
And meet their raging fellows on the hill-tops,
    And we are in the midst.
This beating heart, enriched with the hands' blood,
Stands in the midst and feels the slow joy burn
In solitude and silence, while all about
The gusts clamour like living, crying birds
And the gorse seems hardly tethered to the ground.
    Blow louder, wind, about
My square-set house, rattle the windows, lift
The trap-door to the loft above my head

And let it fall, clapping. Yell in the trees
And throw the rotted oak-bough to the ground,
Flog the dry trailers of my climbing rose—
Make deep, O wind, my rest!

EDWARD SHANKS

5. *To the Thawing Wind*

Come with rain, O loud Southwester!
Bring the singer, bring the nester;
Give the buried flower a dream;
Make the settled snowbank steam;
Find the brown beneath the white;
But whate'er you do tonight,
Bathe my window, make it flow,
Melt it as the ice will go;
Melt the glass and leave the sticks
Like a hermit's crucifix;
Burst into my narrow stall;
Swing the picture on the wall;
Run the rattling pages o'er;
Scatter poems on the floor;
Turn the poet out of door.

ROBERT FROST

6. *Gale Warning*

The wind breaks bound, tossing the oak and chestnut,
Whirling the paper at street corners,
The city clerks are harassed, wrestling head-down:
The gulls are blown inland.

Three slates fall from a roof,
The promenade is in danger:
Inland, the summer fête is postponed,
The British glider record broken.

The wind blows through the City, cleansing,
Whipping the posters from the hoardings,
Tearing the bunting and the banner,
The wind blows steadily, and as it will.

MICHAEL ROBERTS

IX
LET IT RAIN

1. *The Rainy Summer*

There's much afoot in heaven and earth this year;
   The winds hunt up the sun, hunt up the moon,
Trouble the dubious dawn, hasten the drear
   Height of a threatening noon.

No breath of boughs, no breath of leaves, of fronds,
   May linger or grow warm; the trees are loud;
The forest, rooted, tosses in her bonds,
   And strains against the cloud.

No scents may pause within the garden-fold;
   The rifled flowers are cold as ocean-shells;
Bees, humming in the storm, carry their cold
   Wild honey to cold cells.

ALICE MEYNELL

2. *A Sudden Squall*

After some days of heat
Withering leaf and bloom,
Like pebbles falls the hail
Like chips of stone the sleet
Out of the sudden gloom
Across the peaceful vale
Just now so bright.

While we are waiting for
The sulky storm to stop
Hour after hour,
Watching the garden lake
Toss the toy ship,
The orchard fast grows dark
And bruised fruits drop.

Birds are all flown;
Rabbits in holes
Wait for the sun's return;
At sea great whales
Send up their fountains
As they drive taciturn
Through waves like mountains.

Green becomes sodden grey
And across the fields
At death of day
Mist draws her chilly sheets;
Then darkness wields
Its eerie power, night's
Creatures begin to cry.

This weather's change is blind.
His hopes grow dimmer
Who thought that summer
Would never end;
Would have good reason
To change this mind
For a rainy season.

DAVID GASCOYNE

3. Weathers

This is the weather the cuckoo likes,
　　And so do I;
When showers betumble the chestnut spikes,
　　And nestlings fly:
And the little brown nightingale bills his best,
And they sit outside at 'The Travellers' Rest',
And maids come forth sprig-muslin drest,
And citizens dream of the south and west,
　　And so do I.

This is the weather the shepherd shuns,
       And so do I;
When beeches drip in browns and duns,
       And thresh, and ply;
And hill-hid tides throb, throe on throe,
And meadow rivulets overflow,
And drops on gate-bars hang in a row,
And rooks in families homeward go,
       And so do I.

THOMAS HARDY

4. *Flood*

The lingering clouds, rolling, rolling,
And the settled rain, dripping, dripping,
In the Eight Directions—the same dusk.
The level lands—one great river.
Wine I have, wine I have:
Idly I drink at the eastern window.
Longingly—I think of my friends,
But neither boat nor carriage comes.

T'AO CH'IEN
Translated by ARTHUR WALEY

5. *Three Young Rats*

Three young rats with black felt hats,
Three young ducks with white straw flats.[1]
Three young dogs with curling tails,
Three young cats with demi-veils,
Went out to walk with three young pigs
In satin vests and sorrel wigs.
But suddenly it chanced to rain,
And so they all went home again.

ANON

[1] Sandals.

6. *The Storm*

We wake to hear the storm come down,
    Sudden on roof and pane;
The thunder's loud and the hasty wind
    Hurries the beating rain.

The rain slackens, the wind blows gently,
    The gust grows gentle and stills,
And the thunder, like a breaking stick,
    Stumbles about the hills.

The crops still hang on leaf and thorn,
    The downs stand up more green;
The sun comes out again in power
    And the sky is washed and clean.

EDWARD SHANKS

7. From *Evening*

The great rain is over,
    The little rain begun,
Falling from the higher leaves,
    Bright in the sun,
Down to the lower leaves,
    One drop by one.

MARY COLERIDGE

X

SNOWFLAKE AND FALL

1. The Snowflake

Before I melt,
Come, look at me!
This lovely icy filigree!
Of a great forest
In one night
I make a wilderness
Of white:
By skyey cold
Of crystals made,
All softly, on
Your finger laid,
I pause, that you
My beauty see:
Breathe, and I vanish
Instantly.

WALTER DE LA MARE

2. To a Snowflake

What heart could have thought you?—
Past our devisal
(O filigree petal!)
Fashioned so purely,
Fragilely, surely,
From what Paradisal
Imagineless metal,
Too costly for cost?
Who hammered you, wrought you,
From argentine vapour?—
'God was my shaper.
Passing surmisal,
He hammered, He wrought me,
From curled silver vapour,

To lust of His mind:—
Thou could'st not have thought me!
So purely, so palely,
Tinily, surely,
Mightily, frailly,
Insculped and embossed,
With His hammer of wind,
And His graver of frost.'

FRANCIS THOMPSON

3. Snow

A pure white mantle blotted out
    The world I used to know:
There was no scarlet in the sky
    Or on the hills below,
Gently as mercy out of heaven
    Came down the healing snow.

The trees that were so dark and bare
    Stood up in radiant white,
And the road forgot its furrowed care
    As day forgets the night,
And the new heavens and the new earth
    Lay robed in dazzling light.

And every flake that fell from heaven
    Was like an angel's kiss,
Or a feather fluttering from the wings
    Of some dear soul in bliss
Who gently leaned from that bright world
    To soothe the pain of this.

Oft had I felt for some brief flash
    The heavenly secret glow
In sunsets, traced some hieroglyph
    In Nature—flowers that blow
And perish; tender, climbing boughs;
    The stars—and then—'twould go.

But here I felt within my soul,
　　Clear as on field and tree,
The falling of the heavenly snow,
　　A twofold mystery,
And one was meant to bless the world,
　　And one was meant for me.

ALFRED NOYES

4. From *Snow*

Out of the grey air grew snow and more snow
Soundlessly in nonillions of flakes
Commingling and sinking negligently
To ground, soft as froth and easy as ashes
Alighting, closing the ring of sight. And,
Silting, it augmented everything,
Furring the bare leaf, blurring the thorn,
Fluffing, too, the telephone wire, padding
All the paths and boosting boots, and puffing
Big over rims, like boiling milk, meekly
Indulging the bulging hill, and boldly
Bolstering the retiring hole, until
It owned and integrated all. And then
Snow stopped, disclosing anonymity
Imposed, the blank and blotless sea in which
Both dotted tree and dashing bird were sunk,
And anchored ground and rocking grass engrossed.

W. R. RODGERS

5. On a Snow Storm

See! cherubs drop their feathers from their wings,
And hawthorn twigs resume their blossomings.

EDWARD CAPERN

6. *Snow in the Suburbs*

Every branch big with it,
　Bent every twig with it;
Every fork like a white web-foot;
Every street and pavement mute:
Some flakes have lost their way, and grope back upward, when
Meeting those meandering down they turn and descend again.
　The palings are glued together like a wall,
　And there is no waft of wind with the fleecy fall.

　A sparrow enters the tree,
　　Whereon immediately
　A snow-lump thrice his own slight size
　Descends on him and showers his head and eyes.
　　And overturns him,
　　And near inurns him,
　And lights on a nether twig, when its brush
Starts off a volley of other lodging lumps with a rush.

　The steps are a blanched slope,
　　Up which, with feeble hope,
　A black cat comes, wide-eyed and thin;
　　And we take him in.

THOMAS HARDY

7. *Winter*

Snow wind-whipt to ice
Under a hard sun:
Stream-runnels curdled hoar
Crackle, cannot run.

Robin stark dead on twig,
    Song stiffened in it:
Fluffed feathers may not warm
    Bone-thin linnet:

Big-eyed rabbit, lost,
    Scrabbles the snow,
Searching for long-dead grass
    With frost-bit toe:

Mad-tired on the road
    Old Kelly goes;
Through crookt fingers snuffs the air
    Knife-cold in his nose.

Hunger-weak, snow-dazzled,
    Old Thomas Kelly
Thrusts his bit hands, for warmth,
    'Twixt waistcoat and belly.

RICHARD HUGHES

8. *Last Snow*

Although the snow still lingers
Heaped on the ivy's blunt webbed fingers
And painting tree-trunks on one side,
Here in this sunlit ride
The fresh unchristened things appear,
Leaf, spathe and stem,
With crumbs of earth clinging to them

To show the way they came
But no flower yet to tell their name,
And one green spear
Stabbing a dead leaf from below
Kills winter at a blow.

ANDREW YOUNG

AFTERNOON'S AMAZEMENT

I

THE
WORLD OF PEOPLE

1. *The Gardener* from *Novelettes*

He was not able to read or write,
He did odd jobs on gentlemen's places
Cutting the hedge or hoeing the drive
With the smile of a saint,
With the pride of a feudal chief,
For he was not quite all there.

Crippled by rheumatism
By the time his hair was white,
He would reach the garden by twelve
His legs in soiled puttees,
A clay pipe in his teeth,
A tiny flag in his cap
A white cat behind him,
And his eyes a cornflower blue.

And between the clack of the shears
Or the honing of the scythe
Or the rattle of the rake on the gravel
He would talk to amuse the children,
He would talk to amuse himself or the cat
Or the robin waiting for worms
Perched on the handle of the spade;
Would remember snatches of verse
From the elementary school
About a bee and a wasp
Or the cat by the barndoor spinning;
And would talk about himself forever—
You would never find his like—
Always in the third person;
And would level his stick like a gun
(With a glint in his eye)
Saying 'Now I'm a Frenchman'—
He was not quite right in the head.

He believed in God—
The Good Fellow Up There—
And he used a simile of Homer
Watching the fallen leaves,
And every year he waited for the Twelfth of July,
Cherishing his sash and fife
For the carnival of banners and drums.
He was always claiming but never
Obtaining his old age pension,
For he did not know his age.
And his rheumatism at last
Kept him out of the processions.

And he came to work in the garden
Later and later in the day,
Leaving later at night;
In the damp dark of the night
At ten o'clock or later
You could hear him mowing the lawn,
The mower moving forward,
And backward, forward and backward
For he mowed while standing still;
He was not quite up to the job.

But he took a pride in the job,
He kept a bowl of cold
Tea in the crotch of a tree,
Always enjoyed his food
And enjoying honing the scythe
And making the potato drills
And putting the peasticks in;
And enjoyed the noise of the corncrake,
And the early hawthorn hedge
Peppered black and green,
And the cut grass dancing in the air—
Happy as the day was long.

Till his last sickness took him
And he could not leave his house
And his eyes lost their colour
And he sat by the little range
With a finch in a cage and a framed
Certificate of admission
Into the Orange Order,
And his speech began to wander
And memory ebbed
Leaving upon the shore
Odd shells and heaps of wrack
And his soul went out with the ebbing
Tide in a trim boat
To find the Walls of Derry
Or the land of the Ever Young.

LOUIS MACNEICE

2. From *The Rural Postman*

O, the postman's is as pleasant a life
    As any one's, I trow;
For day by day he wendeth his way,
    Where a thousand wildings grow.
He marketh the date of the snowdrop's birth,
    And knows when the time is near
For white scented violets to gladden the earth,
    And sweet primrose groups t' appear.
He can show you the spot where the hyacinth wild
    Hangs out her bell blossoms o' blue;
And tell where the celandine's bright-eyed child
    Fills her chalice with honey dew.
The purple-dyed violet, the hawthorn, and sloe,
    The creepers that trail in the lane,
The dragon, the daisy, the clover-rose, too,
    And buttercups gilding the plain;

The foxglove, the robert, the gorse and the thyme,
  The heather and broom on the moor,
And the sweet honey-suckle that loveth to climb
  The arch of the cottager's door.
He knoweth them all, and he loveth them well,
  And others not honour'd with fame,
For they hang round his life like a beautiful spell,
  And light up his path with their flame.
O, a pleasant life is the postman's life
  And a fine cheerful soul is he,
For he'll shout and sing like a forest king,
  On the crown of an ancient tree.

Heigho! I come and go,
Where the Lent lily, speedwell and dog-rose blow,
Heigho! and merry, O!
  Where hawkweeds, and trefoils, and wild peas grow.
Heigho! Heigho!
  As pleasant as May-time, as light as a roe.

EDWARD CAPERN

3. The Poet's Song

The rain had fallen, the Poet arose,
  He pass'd by the town and out of the street,
A light wind blew from the gates of the sun,
  And waves of shadow went over the wheat,
And he sat him down in a lonely place,
  And chanted a melody loud and sweet,
That made the wild-swan pause in her cloud,
  And the lark drop down at his feet.

The swallow stopt as he hunted the bee,
  The snake slipt under a spray,
The wild hawk stood with the down on his beak,
  And stared, with his foot on the prey,

And the nightingale thought, 'I have sung many songs,
    But never a one so gay,
For he sings of what the world will be
    When the years have died away.'

ALFRED, LORD TENNYSON

4. Pollie

Pollie is a simpleton,
'Look!' she cries, 'that *lovely* swan!'
And, even before her transports cease,
    Adds, 'But I do love geese.'

When a lark wings up the sky,
She'll sit with her lips ajar, then sigh—
For rapture; and the rapture o'er,
    Whisper, 'What's music *for*?'

Every lesson I allot,
As soon as learned is clean forgot.
'L—O—V. . . ?' I prompt. And she
    Smiles, but I catch no 'E'.

It seems in her round head you come
As if to a secret vacuum;
Whence then the wonder, love and grace
    Shining in that small face?

WALTER DE LA MARE

5. The Fiddler of Dooney

When I play on my fiddle in Dooney,
Folk dance like a wave of the sea;
My cousin is priest in Kilvarnet,
My brother in Mocharabuiee.

I passed by my brother and cousin:
They read in their books of prayer;
I read in my book of songs
I bought at the Sligo fair.

When we come at the end of time
To Peter sitting in state,
He will smile on the three old spirits,
But call me first through the gate;

For the good are always merry,
Save by an evil chance,
And the merry love the fiddle,
And the merry love to dance:

And when the folk there spy me,
They will all come up to me,
With 'Here is the fiddler of Dooney!'
And dance like a wave of the sea.

W. B. YEATS

6. Skipper

(Of the clipper ship Mary Ambree)

A rough old nut,
A tough old nut
Of a skipper:
But the right stuff,
Sure enough,
   For a racing clipper.

Stiff and sturdy and five foot seven—
Cares for nobody under heaven;
All a-taut-o from truck to keel,
Will like iron and nerves like steel:
Loves his old packet better'n his life,
Loves her like sweetheart, or child, or wife:
Runs down the easting under all she'll carry,
Hates taking sail off her worse'n Old Harry!

When winds are baffling or Trades are slack,
Or she's beating to windward tack and tack,
And the most she's logging is nine or ten,
He's the devil and all to live with then.
He curses the watch and he rows the mates,
Gives steward the jumps till he smashes the plates,
And nibbles his nails, and damns the weather,
And wishes the lot at the deuce together.

But oh! it's a different sort of tale
When the seventeenth knot is over the rail,
With the Forties roaring their blooming best,
And the big seas galloping out of the West,
And the packet rolling her lee-rail under
And shipping it green with a noise like thunder,
And the galley's swamped, and the half-deck's drowned,
And the pots and kettles are swimming around,
And she's romping through it with all she'll stand—
Oh, everything in the garden's grand!
He'll walk the poop, and he'll whistle and sing
As happy and proud as a blooming king,
And he licks his chops, the hoary old sinner,
Like the cabin cat when there's fish for dinner,
And says, as he holds by the weather shrouds
And squints aloft at the hurrying clouds:
'Mister, I reckon it's time, about,
We shook them reefs in her topsails out!'

C. FOX SMITH

7. Mrs Malone

Mrs Malone
Lived hard by a wood
All on her lonesome
As nobody should.
With her crust on a plate
And her pot on the coal
And none but herself
To converse with, poor soul.

In a shawl and a hood
She got sticks out-o'-door,
On a bit of old sacking
She slept on the floor,
And nobody, nobody
Asked how she fared
Or knew how she managed,
For nobody cared.

    Why make a pother
    About an old crone?
    What for should they bother
    With Mrs Malone?

One Monday in winter
With snow on the ground
So thick that a footstep
Fell without sound,
She heard a faint frostbitten
Peck on the pane
And went to the window
To listen again.
There sat a cock-sparrow
Bedraggled and weak,
With half-open eyelid
And ice on its beak.
She threw up the sash
And she took the bird in,
And mumbled and fumbled it
Under her chin.

    'Ye're all of a smother,
    Ye're fair overblown!
    I've room fer another,'
    Said Mrs Malone.

Come Tuesday while eating
Her dry morning slice
With the sparrow a-picking
('Ain't company nice!')
She heard on her doorpost

A curious scratch,
And there was a cat
With its claw on the latch.
It was hungry and thirsty
And thin as a lath,
It mewed and it mowed
On the slithery path.
She threw the door open
And warmed up some pap,
And huddled and cuddled it
In her old lap.
          'There, there, little brother,
          Ye poor skin-an'-bone,
          There's room fer another,'
          Said Mrs Malone.

Come Wednesday while all of them
Crouched on the mat
With a crumb for the sparrow,
A sip for the cat,
There was wailing and whining
Outside in the wood,
And there sat a vixen
With six of her brood.
She was haggard and ragged
And worn to a shred,
And her half-dozen babies
Were only half fed,
But Mrs Malone, crying
'My! ain't they sweet!'
Happed them and lapped them
And gave them to eat.
          'You warm yerself, mother
          Ye're cold as a stone!
          There's room for another,'
          Said Mrs Malone.

Come Thursday a donkey
Stepped in off the road
With sores on its withers
From bearing a load.
Come Friday when icicles
Pierced the white air
Down from the mountainside
Lumbered a bear.
For each she had something,
If little, to give—
'Lord knows, the poor critters
Must all of 'em live.'
She gave them her sacking,
Her hood and her shawl,
Her loaf and her teapot—
She gave them her all.
      'What with one thing and t'other
      Me fambily's grown,
      And there's room fer another,'
      Said Mrs Malone.

Come Saturday evening
When time was to sup
Mrs Malone
Had forgot to sit up.
The cat said *meeow*,
The sparrow said *peep*,
The vixen, *she's sleeping*,
The bear, *let her sleep*.
On the back of the donkey
They bore her away,
Through trees and up mountains
Beyond night and day,
Till come Sunday morning
They brought her in state
Through the last cloudbank
As far as the Gate.

'Who is it?' asked Peter,
'You have with you there?'
And donkey and sparrow,
Cat, vixen and bear

Exclaimed, 'Do you tell us
Up here she's unknown?
It's our mother, God bless us!
It's Mrs Malone
Whose havings were few
And whose holding was small
And whose heart was so big
It had room for us all.'
Then Mrs Malone
Of a sudden awoke,
She rubbed her two eyeballs
And anxiously spoke:
'Where am I, to goodness,
And what do I see?
My dears, let's turn back,
This ain't no place for me!'
But Peter said, 'Mother
Go in to the Throne.
There's room for another
One, Mrs Malone.'

ELEANOR FARJEON

8. *Meg Merrilies*

Old Meg she was a Gipsey,
    And liv'd upon the Moors;
Her bed it was the brown heath turf,
    And her house was out of doors.

Her apples were swart blackberries,
    Her currants, pods o' broom;
Her wine was dew of the wild white rose,
    Her book a churchyard tomb.

Her Brothers were the craggy hills,
  Her Sisters larchen trees;
Alone with her great family
  She liv'd as she did please.

No breakfast had she many a morn,
  No dinner many a noon,
And, 'stead of supper, she would stare
  Full hard against the Moon.

But every morn, of woodbine fresh
  She made her garlanding,
And, every night, the dark glen Yew
  She wove, and she would sing.

And with her fingers, old and brown,
  She plaited Mats o' Rushes,
And gave them to the Cottagers
  She met among the Bushes.

Old Meg was brave as Margaret Queen
  And tall as Amazon;
An old red blanket cloak she wore,
  A chip hat had she on.
God rest her aged bones somewhere!
  She died full long agone!

JOHN KEATS

II
TRAVELLERS

1. Kiph

My Uncle Ben, who's been
To Bisk, Bhir, Biak—
Been, and come back:
To Tab, Tau, Tze, and Tomsk,
And home, by Teneriffe:
Who, brown as desert sand,
Gaunt, staring, slow and stiff,
Has chased the Unicorn
And Hippogriff,
Gave me a smooth, small shining stone,
Called *Kiph*.

'Look'ee, now, Nevvy mine,'
He told me—'*If*
You'd wish a wish,
Just rub this smooth, small, shining stone,
Called *Kiph*.'

Hide it did I,
In a safe, secret spot;
Slept, and the place
In dreams forgot.

One wish *alone*
Now's mine: Oh, if
I could but find again
That stone called *Kiph*!

WALTER DE LA MARE

2. The Vagabond

Give to me the life I love,
    Let the lave go by me,
Give the jolly heaven above
    And the byway nigh me.

136

Bed in the bush with the stars to see,
 Bread I dip in the river—
There's the life for a man like me,
 There's the life for ever.

Let the blow fall soon or late,
 Let what will be o'er me;
Give the face of earth around
 And the road before me.
Wealth I seek not, hope nor love,
 Nor a friend to know me;
All I seek, the heaven above
 And the road below me.

Or let autumn fall on me
 Where afield I linger,
Silencing the bird on tree,
 Biting the blue finger.
White as meal the frosty field—
 Warm the fireside haven—
Not to autumn will I yield,
 Not to winter even!

Let the blow fall soon or late,
 Let what will be o'er me;
Give the face of earth around,
 And the road before me;
Wealth I ask not, hope nor love,
 Nor a friend to know me;
All I ask the heaven above,
 And the road below me.

ROBERT LOUIS STEVENSON

3. Walking Song

Here we go a-walking, so softly, so softly,
 Down the world, round the world, back to London town,
To see the waters and the whales, the emus and the mandarins,
 To see the Chinese mandarins, each in a silken gown.

Here we go a-walking, so softly, so softly,
    Out by holy Glastonbury, back to London town,
Before a cup, a shining cup, a cup of beating crimson,
    To see Saint Joseph saying mass all with a shaven crown.

And round him are the silly things of hoof and claw and
        feather,
    Upon his right the farmyard, upon his left the wild;
All the lambs of all the folds bleat out the Agnus Dei,
    And when he says the holy words he holds the Holy
        Child.

Here we go a-walking, so softly, so softly,
    Through the vast Atlantic waves, back to London town,
To see the ships made whole again that sank below the
        tempest,
    The Trojan and Phoenician ships that long ago went
        down.

And there are sailors keeping watch on many a Roman galley,
    And silver bars and golden bars and mighty treasure hid,
And splendid Spanish gentlemen majestically walking
    And waiting on their admiral as once in far Madrid.

Here we go a-walking, so softly, so softly,
    Down and under to New York, back to London town,
To see the face of Liberty that smiles upon all children,
    But when too soon they come to age she answers with
        a frown.

And there are all the dancing stars beside the toppling
        windows,
    Human lights and heavenly lights they twinkle side by
        side;
There is passing through the streets the mighty voice of
        Jefferson
    And the armies of George Washington who would not be
        denied.

Here we go a-walking, so softly, so softly,
O'er the wide Tibetan plains, back to London town,
To see the youthful Emperor among his seventy princes,
Who bears the mystic sceptre, who wears the mystic crown.

The tongue he speaks is older far than Hebrew or than Latin,
And ancient rituals drawn therein his eyes of mercy con;
About his throne the candles shine and thuribles of incense
Are swung about his footstool, and his name is Prester John.

Here we go a-walking, so softly, so softly,
Down the pass of Himalay, back to London town,
To see our lord most pitiful, the holy Prince of Siddartha,
And the Peacock Throne of Akbar, the great Timur riding down.

Up to Delhi, up to Delhi! lo the Mogul's glory,
Twice ten thousand elephants trumpet round his tent;
Down from Delhi, down from Delhi! lo the leafy budh-tree
Where our lord at the fourth watch achieved enlightenment.

Here we go a-walking, so softly, so softly,
Through the jungles African, back to London town,
To see the shining rivers and the drinking-place by moonlight,
And the lions and hyenas and the zebras coming down:

To see bright birds and butterflies, the monstrous hippopotami,
The silent secret crocodiles that keep their ancient guile,
The white road of the caravans that stretches o'er Sahara,
And the Pharaoh in his litter at the fording of the Nile.

Here we go a-walking, so softly, so softly,
Up the holy streets of Rome, back to London town,
To see the marching legions and the Consuls in their triumph,
And the moving lips of Virgil and the laurel of his crown:

139

And there is Caesar pacing to the foot of Pompey's statue,
  All scornful of his mastery, all careless of alarms;
And there the Pope goes all in white among his scarlet
    Cardinals
  And carried on the shoulders of his gentlemen-at-arms.

Here we go a-walking, so softly, so softly,
  Up the hills of Hampstead, back to London town,
And the garden gate stands open and the house door swings
    before us,
  And the candles twinkle happily as we lie down.

For here the noble lady is who meets us from our wanderings,
  Here are all the sensible and very needful things,
Here are blankets, here is milk, here are rest and slumber,
    And the courteous prince of angels with the fire about
    his wings.

CHARLES WILLIAMS

4. *Romance*

When I was but thirteen or so
    I went into a golden land,
Chimborazo, Cotopaxi
    Took me by the hand.

My father died, my brother too,
    They passed like fleeting dreams.
I stood where Popocatapetl
    In the sunlight gleams.

I dimly heard the master's voice
    And boys' far-off at play,
Chimborazo, Cotopaxi
    Had stolen me away.

I walked in a great golden dream
    To and fro from school—
Shining Popocatapetl
    The dusty streets did rule.

I walked home with a gold dark boy
    And never a word I'd say,
Chimborazo, Cotopaxi
    Had taken my speech away:

I gazed entranced upon his face
    Fairer than any flower—
O shining Popocatapetl
    It was thy magic hour:

The houses, people, traffic seemed
    Thin fading dreams by day,
Chimborazo, Cotopaxi
    They had stolen my soul away!

W. J. TURNER

5. Bermudas

Where the remote Bermudas ride
In th' Ocean's bosom unespi'd,
From a small boat, that row'd along,
The listening winds receiv'd this song.
'What should we do but sing His praise
That led us through the watery maze,
Unto an isle so long unknown,
And yet far kinder than our own?
Where He the huge sea-monsters wracks,
That lift the deep upon their backs.
He lands us on a grassy stage;
Safe from the storms and prelate's rage.
He gave us this eternal Spring,
Which here enamels every thing:
And sends the fowls to us in care,
On daily visits through the air.
He hangs in shades the orange bright,
Like golden lamps in a green night.
And does in the pomegranates close,
Jewels more rich than Ormus shows.

He makes the figs our mouths to meet;
And throws the melons at our feet.
But apples plants of such a price,
No tree could ever bear them twice.
With cedars, chosen by His hand,
From Lebanon, He stores the land.
And makes the hollow seas, that roar,
Proclaim the ambergris on shore.
He cast (of which we rather boast)
The Gospel's pearl upon our coast.
And in these rocks for us did frame
A temple, where to sound His name.
Oh! let our voice His praise exalt,
Till it arrive at Heaven's vault:
Which thence (perhaps) rebounding, may
Echo beyond the Mexique Bay.'
Thus sang they, in the English boat,
A holy and a cheerful note,
And all the way, to guide their chime,
With falling oars they kept the time.

ANDREW MARVELL

6. *Idle Thoughts*

Sing of romantic palaces
In Tripoli, in Tripoli,
Above the sighing and the surge
Of the moaning sea, the slothful sea;
Of palaces upon the verge
Of the languid sea, the sleepy sea.

Sing of romantic palaces
In Venice by the broad lagoons
With hoodwink mask and domino,
With cupolas like cuspèd moons
In waters dim reflected glow,
And ghosts of stately frigatoons
In dusky waters come and go.

Sing of romantic palaces
In cities set by gilded seas,
Slenderly mimicking in waves
The lace of spires and balconies,
The oriels and the architraves,
—Dreams! dreams! where lead such dreams as these?

V. SACKVILLE-WEST

7. Kingdoms

The sailor tells the children
　　His stories of the sea,
Their eyes look over the water
　　To where his wonders be:

The flowers as big as tea-cups,
　　The great big butterflies
The long unfooted beaches
　　Where stored-up treasure lies.

More than a thousand islands
　　Each curved around its pool:
All kingdoms filled with sunlight,
　　Where no one goes to school;

The fish that leave the water
　　In sudden bends of light
The birds as blue as china;
　　The flies that gleam by night . . „

Till, slowly, I remember
　　A wistful place; and then,—
The story of that Kingdom
　　First told to longshoremen.

OLIVER ST JOHN GOGARTY

8. *Mamble*

I never went to Mamble
That lies above the Teme,
So I wonder who's in Mamble,
And whether people seem
Who breed and brew along there
As lazy as the name,
And whether any song there
Sets alehouse wits aflame.

The finger-post says Mamble,
And that is all I know
Of the narrow road to Mamble,
And should I turn and go
To that place of lazy token,
That lies above the Teme,
There might be a Mamble broken
That was lissom in a dream.

So leave the road to Mamble
And take another road
To as good a place as Mamble
Be it lazy as a toad;
Who travels Worcester county
Takes any place that comes
When April tosses bounty
To the cherries and the plums.

JOHN DRINKWATER

9. *Young and Old*

When all the world is young, lad,
    And all the trees are green;
And every goose a swan, lad,
    And every lass a queen;

144

Then hey for boot and horse, lad,
    And round the world away:
Young blood must have its course, lad,
    And every dog his day.

When all the world is old, lad,
    And all the trees are brown;
And all the sport is stale, lad,
    And all the wheels run down;
Creep home, and take your place there,
    The spent and maimed among:
God grant you find one face there,
    You loved when all was young.

CHARLES KINGSLEY

III
RAILWAY LINES

1. The Express

After the first powerful plain manifesto
The black statement of pistons, without more fuss
But gliding like a queen, she leaves the station.
Without bowing and with restrained unconcern
She passes the houses which humbly crowd outside,
The gasworks and at last the heavy page
Of death, printed by gravestones in the cemetery.
Beyond the town there lies the open country
Where, gathering speed, she acquires mystery,
The luminous self-possession of ships on ocean.
It is now she begins to sing—at first quite low
Then loud, and at last with a jazzy madness—
The song of her whistle screaming at curves,
Of deafening tunnels, brakes, innumerable bolts.
And always light, aerial, underneath
Goes the elate metre of her wheels.
Steaming through metal landscape on her lines
She plunges new eras of wild happiness
Where speed throws up strange shapes, broad curves
And parallels clean like the steel of guns.
At last, further than Edinburgh or Rome,
Beyond the crest of the world, she reaches night
Where only a low streamline brightness
Of phosphorus on the tossing hills is white.
Ah, like a comet through flame, she moves entranced
Wrapt in her music no bird song, no, nor bough
Breaking with honey buds, shall ever equal.

STEPHEN SPENDER

2. Night Mail

This is the night mail crossing the border,
Bringing the cheque and the postal order,
Letters for the rich, letters for the poor,
The shop at the corner and the girl next door.
Pulling up Beattock, a steady climb—
The gradient's against her, but she's on time.

Past cotton grass and moorland boulder
Shovelling white steam over her shoulder,
Snorting noisily as she passes
Silent miles of wind-bent grasses.

Birds turn their heads as she approaches,
Stare from the bushes at her black-faced coaches.
Sheep-dogs cannot turn her course,
They slumber on with paws across.
In the farm she passes no one wakes,
But a jug in the bedroom gently shakes.

Dawn freshens, the climb is done.
Down towards Glasgow she descends
Towards the steam tugs yelping down the glade of cranes,
Towards the fields of apparatus, the furnaces
Set on the dark plain like gigantic chessmen.
All Scotland waits for her:
In the dark glens, beside the pale-green lochs
Men long for news.

Letters of thanks, letters from banks,
Letters of joy from girl and boy,
Receipted bills and invitations
To inspect new stock or visit relations,
And applications for situations
And timid lovers' declarations
And gossip, gossip from all the nations,
News circumstantial, news financial,
Letters with holiday snaps to enlarge in,
Letters with faces scrawled in the margin,
Letters from uncles, cousins, and aunts,
Letters to Scotland from the South of France,
Letters of condolence to Highlands and Lowlands,
Notes from overseas to Hebrides—

Written on paper of every hue,
The pink, the violet, the white and the blue,

The chatty, the catty, the boring, adoring,
The cold and official and the heart outpouring,
Clever, stupid, short and long,
The typed and printed and the spelt all wrong.

Thousands are still asleep
Dreaming of terrifying monsters,
Or of friendly tea beside the band at Cranston's or Crawford's.
Asleep in working Glasgow, asleep in well-set Edinburgh,
Asleep in granite Aberdeen,
They continue their dreams;
And shall wake soon and long for letters,
And none will hear the postman's knock
Without a quickening of the heart,
For who can hear and feel himself forgotten?

W. H. AUDEN

3. From a Railway Carriage

Faster than fairies, faster than witches,
Bridges and houses, hedges and ditches;
And charging along like troops in a battle,
All through the meadows the horses and cattle:
All of the sights of the hill and the plain
Fly as thick as driving rain;
And ever again, in the wink of an eye,
Painted stations whistle by.

Here is a child who clambers and scrambles,
All by himself and gathering brambles;
Here is a tramp who stands and gazes;
And there is the green for stringing the daisies!
Here is a cart run away in the road
Lumping along with man and load;
And here is a mill and there is a river:
Each a glimpse and gone for ever!

ROBERT LOUIS STEVENSON

4. *The Child in the Train*

The train stands still
    And the world runs by.
Yonder runs a tree
    And a cloud in the sky.
Here flies a pony
    On the running road,
And there flows the quickest
    River ever flowed.

The mountains on the edge
    Roll away like the tide,
The backs of the houses
    Pass on a slide,
The little farms slip off
    As soon as one looks,
And the little churches vanish
    With their spires and their rooks.

The buttercup embankments,
    The telegraph wires,
The names of the stations,
    The small heath fires,
The hoardings in the fields,
    And the people in the street,
Go whizzing into somewhere
    While I keep my seat.

The little cities trot,
    And the little hamlets trip,
The meadow with its cow,
    The sea with its ship,
The forest and the factory,
    The hedge and the hill—
The world goes running by
    While the train stands still!

ELEANOR FARJEON

5. From *Journey*

Oh the wild engine! Every time I sit
In a train I must remember it.
The way it smashes through the air; its great
Petulant majesty and terrible rate:
Driving the ground before it, with those round
Feet pounding, beating, covering the ground;
The piston using up the white steam so
You cannot watch it when it come or go;
The cutting, the embankment; how it takes
The tunnels, and the clatter that it makes;
So careful of the train and of the track,
Guiding us out, or helping us go back;
Breasting its destination: at the close
Yawning, and slowly dropping to a doze.

HAROLD MONRO

6. *Out of the Window*

In the middle of countries, far from hills and sea,
Are the little places one passes by in trains
And never stops at; where the skies extend
Uninterrupted, and the level plains
Stretch green and yellow and green without an end.
And behind the glass of their Grand Express
Folk yawn away a province through,
With nothing to think of, nothing to do,
Nothing even to look at—never a 'view'
In this damned wilderness.
But I look out of the window and find
Much to satisfy the mind.
Mark how the furrows, formed and wheeled
In a motion orderly and staid,
Sweep, as we pass, across the field
Like a drilled army on parade.

And here's a market-garden, barred
With stripe on stripe of varied greens . . .
Bright potatoes, flower starred,
And the opacous colour of beans.
Each line deliberately swings
Towards me, till I see a straight
Green avenue to the heart of things,
The glimpse of a sudden opened gate
Piercing the adverse walls of fate . . .
A moment only, and then, fast, fast,
The gate swings to, the avenue closes;
Fate laughs, and once more interposes
Its barriers.
        The train has passed.

ALDOUS HUXLEY

7. *Adlestrop*

Yes. I remember Adlestrop—
The name, because one afternoon
Of heat the express-train drew up there
Unwontedly. It was late June.

The steam hissed. Someone cleared his throat.
No one left and no one came
On the bare platform. What I saw
Was Adlestrop—only the name

And willows, willow-herb, and grass,
And meadowsweet, and haycocks dry,
No whit less still and lonely fair
Than the high cloudlets in the sky.

And for that minute a blackbird sang
Close by, and round him, mistier,
Farther and farther, all the birds
Of Oxfordshire and Gloucestershire.

EDWARD THOMAS

152

IV

SPLENDID SHIPS

1. The Ship

They have launched the little ship,
    She is riding by the quay.
Like a young doe to the river,
    She has trembled to the sea.

Her sails are shaken loose;
    They flutter in the wind.
The cat's-paws ripple round her
    And the gulls scream behind.

The rope is cast, she moves
    Daintily out and south,
Where the snarling ocean waits her
    With tiger-foaming mouth.

RICHARD CHURCH

2. A Passer-by

Whither, O splendid ship, thy white sails crowding,
    Leaning across the bosom of the urgent West,
That fearest nor sea rising, nor sky clouding,
    Whither away, fair rover, and what thy quest?
    Ah! soon, when Winter has all our vales opprest,
When skies are cold and misty, and hail is hurling,
    Wilt thou glide on the blue Pacific, or rest
In a summer haven asleep, thy white sails furling.

I there before thee, in the country that well thou knowest,
    Already arrived am inhaling the odorous air:
I watch thee enter unerringly where thou goest,
    And anchor queen of the strange shipping there,
    Thy sails for awnings spread, thy masts bare:
Nor is aught from the foaming reef to the snow-capped, grandest
    Peak, that is over the feathery palms more fair
Than thou, so upright, so stately, and still thou standest.

And yet, O splendid ship, unhailed and nameless,
    I know not if, aiming a fancy, I rightly divine
That thou hast a purpose joyful, a courage blameless,
    Thy port assured in a happier land than mine.
    But for all I have given thee, beauty enough is thine,
As thou, aslant with trim tackle and shrouding,
    From the proud nostril curve of a prow's line
In the offing scatterest foam, thy white sails crowding.

ROBERT BRIDGES

3. Sonnet

Where lies the land to which yon ship must go?
Fresh as a lark mounting at break of day,
Festively she puts forth in trim array;
Is she for tropic suns, or polar snow?
What boots the inquiry?—Neither friend nor foe
She cares for; let her travel where she may,
She finds familiar names, a beaten way
Ever before her, and a wind to blow.
Yet still I ask, what haven is her mark?
And, almost as it was when ships were rare,
(From time to time, like pilgrims, here and there
Crossing the waters) doubt, and something dark,
Of the old sea some reverential fear,
Is with me at thy farewell, joyous bark!

WILLIAM WORDSWORTH

4. Where Lies the Land . . .

Where lies the land to which the ship would go?
Far, far ahead, is all her seamen know.
And where the land she travels from? Away,
Far, far behind, is all that they can say.

On sunny noons upon the deck's smooth face,
Linked arm in arm, how pleasant here to pace;
Or, o'er the stern reclining, watch below
The foaming wake far widening as we go.

On stormy nights when wild north-westers rave,
How proud a thing to fight with wind and wave!
The dripping sailor on the reeling mast
Exults to bear, and scorns to wish it past.

Where lies the land to which the ship would go?
Far, far ahead, is all her seamen know.
And where the land she travels from? Away,
Far, far behind, is all that they can say.

ARTHUR HUGH CLOUGH

5. Sailor's Delight

Tall raking clipper ships driving hell-for-leather,
Swinging down the Forties in the easting weather;
Old wooden Indiamen leaking like baskets,
With half their ratlines missing and rotten slings and gaskets:
Big fourposters out of Mersey and Clyde,
Bound for grain to 'Frisco, not to be denied,
Thrashing to the westward through the great Horn seas
With a crowd of husky reefers and a dozen A.B.s . . .

Those were the ships Mike Murphy used to sail in,
Those were the sort he weathered many a gale in,
Handed, reefed and furled in from Timor to the Tongue,
In the old days, the hard days,
The done-with mast and yard days,
(And 'ah, but they were grand days, them days when he was
    young!').

156

Seal oil, whale oil, ivory and grain,
Lumber out of Puget Sound, and wine out of Spain,
Deer's horns and jaggery they used to load at lost
God-forsaken ports on the Coromandel coast . . .
Copra from the South Seas, coal out of Wales,
Copper ore, cinnamon, monkey nuts and nails:
Sweet cloves from Zanzibar, beans from Peru,
And a young white elephant consigned to the Zoo . . .

Those were the freights he sailed the world around with,
Those were the things he's been everything but drowned with,
Scorched and soaked and frozen from Cork to Chittagong,
In the sail days, the old days,
The hungry days, the cold days,
(And 'ah, but they were fine days, them days when he was
    young!').

Hard hairy sailormen with weather-tanned faces,
Hands bent with hauling on sheets, tacks and braces,
Brawny forearms tattooed with strange devices,
And tough fingers skilled in cunning knots and splices . . .
Full of rum yarns and superstitious notions,
And odd bits of lingo from half a dozen oceans,
And many an old shanty, and old sailor song
To while away a dog-watch, twenty verses long . . .

Those were the blokes Mike Murphy went to sea with,
Those were the sort of chaps he used to be with,
Share his trick and whack with, laughed and swore and sung,
In the old days, the tough days,
Salt junk and leathery duff days,
(And 'ah, but them was great days, them days when he was
    young!').

C. FOX SMITH

6. From *Ultima Thule*

With favouring winds, o'er the sunlit seas,
We sailed for the Hesperides,
The land where the golden apples grow;
But that, ah! that was long ago.

How far, since then, the ocean streams
Have swept us from that land of dreams,
That land of fiction and of truth,
The lost Atlantis of our youth!

Whither, ah, whither? Are not these
The tempest-haunted Hebrides,
Where sea-gulls scream, and breakers roar
And wreck and seaweed line the shore?

Ultima Thule! Utmost Isle!
Here in thy harbours for a while
We lower our sails; a while we rest
From the unending, endless quest.

HENRY WADSWORTH LONGFELLOW

7. *Where go the Boats?*

Dark brown is the river,
    Golden is the sand.
It flows along for ever,
    With trees on either hand.

Green leaves a-floating,
    Castles of the foam,
Boats of mine a-boating—
    Where will all come home?

On goes the river
    And out past the mill,
Away down the valley,
    Away down the hill.

Away down the river,
A hundred miles or more,
Other little children
Shall bring my boats to shore.

ROBERT LOUIS STEVENSON

8. From *Paper Boats*

Day by day I float my paper boats one by one down the running stream.

In big black letters I write my name on them and the name of the village where I live.

I hope that someone in some strange land will find them and know who I am.

I load my little boats with *shiuli* flowers from our garden, and hope that these blooms of the dawn will be carried safely to land in the night . . .

RABINDRANATH TAGORE

V

OUT OF THE ARK

1. From *The Flaming Terrapin*

Out of the Ark's grim hold
A torrent of splendour rolled—
From the hollow resounding sides,
Flashing and glittering, came
Panthers with sparkled hides,
And tigers scribbled with flame,
And lions in grisly trains
Cascading their golden manes.
They ramped in the morning light,
And over their stripes and stars
The sun-shot lightnings, quivering bright,
Rippled in zigzag bars.
The wildebeest frisked with the gale
On the crags of a hunchback mountain,
With his heels in the clouds, he flirted his tail
Like the jet of a silvery fountain.
Frail oribi sailed with their golden-skinned
And feathery limbs laid light on the wind.
And the springbok bounced, and fluttered, and
    flew,
Hooped their spines on the gaunt karroo.
Gay zebras pranced and snorted aloud—
With the crackle of hail their hard hoofs pelt,
And thunder breaks from the rolling cloud
That they raise on the dusty Veldt.
O, hark how the rapids of the Congo
Are chanting their rolling strains,
And the sun-dappled herds a-skipping to the song,
    go
Kicking up the dust on the great, grey plains—
Tsessebe, Koodoo, Buffalo, Bongo,
With the fierce wind foaming in their manes.

ROY CAMPBELL

2. The Bat

Lightless, unholy, eldritch thing,
Whose murky and erratic wing
Swoops so sickeningly, and whose
Aspect to the female Muse
Is a demon's, made of stuff
Like tattered, sooty waterproof,
Looking dirty, clammy, cold.

Wicked, poisonous, and old;
I have maligned thee! . . . for the Cat
Lately caught a little bat,
Seized it softly, bore it in.
On the carpet, dark as sin
In the lamplight, painfully
It limped about, and could not fly.

Even fear must yield to love,
And pity make the depths to move.
Though sick with horror, I must stoop,
Grasp it gently, take it up,
And carry it, and place it where
It could resume the twilight air.

Strange revelation! warm as milk,
Clean as a flower, smooth as silk!
O what a piteous face appears,
What great fine thin translucent ears
What chestnut down and crapy wings,
Finer than any lady's things—
And O a little one that clings!

Warm, clean, and lovely, though not fair,
And burdened with a mother's care;
Go hunt the hurtful fly, and bear
My Blessing to your kind in air.

RUTH PITTER

3. A Narrow Fellow in the Grass

A narrow fellow in the grass
Occasionally rides;
You may have met him,—did you not?
His notice sudden is.

The grass divides as with a comb,
A spotted shaft is seen;
And then it closes at your feet
And opens further on.

He likes a boggy acre,
A floor too cool for corn.
Yet when a child, and barefoot,
I more than once, at morn,

Have passed, I thought, a whip-lash
Unbraiding in the sun,—
When, stooping to secure it,
It wrinkled, and was gone.

Several of nature's people
I know, and they know me;
I feel for them a transport
Of cordiality;

But never met this fellow,
Attended or alone,
Without a tighter breathing,
And zero at the bone.

EMILY DICKINSON

4. The Viper

Barefoot I went and made no sound;
The earth was hot beneath:
The air was quivering around,
The circling kestrel eyed the ground
    And hung above the heath.

There in the pathway stretched along
The lovely serpent lay:
She reared not up the heath among,
She bowed her head, she sheathed her tongue,
And shining stole away.

Fair was the brave embroidered dress,
Fairer the gold eyes shone:
Loving her not, yet did I bless
The fallen angel's comeliness;
    And gazed when she had gone.

RUTH PITTER

5. *The Squirrel*

Among the fox-red fallen leaves I surprised him. Snap
up the chestnut bole he leapt,
the brown leaper, clawing up-swept:
turned on the first bough and scolded me roundly.
That's right, load me with reviling,
spit at me, swear horrible, shame me if you can.
But scared of my smiling
off and up he scurries. Now Jack's up the beanstalk
among the dizzy giants. He skips
along the highest branches, along
tree-fingers slender as string,
fur tail following, to the very tips:
then leaps the aisle—
O fear he fall
a hundred times his little length!
He's over! clings, swings on a spray,
then lightly, the ghost of a mouse, against the sky traces
for me his runway of rare wonder, races
helter-skelter without pause or break
(I think of the snail—how long would he take?)
on and onward, not done yet—
his errand? some nut-plunder, you bet.

Oh he's gone!
I peer and search and strain for him, but he's gone.
I wait and watch at the giants' feet, among
the fox-red fallen leaves. One drop
of rain lands with a smart tap
on the drum, on parchment leaf. I wait
and wait and shiver and forget . . .

A fancy: suppose these trees, so ancient, so
venerable, so rock-rooted, suddenly
heaved up their huge elephantine hooves
(O the leaves, how they'd splutter and splash
like a waterfall, a red waterfall)—suppose
they trudged away!
What would the squirrel say?

IAN SERRAILLIER

6. *Lullaby for a Baby Toad*

Sleep, my child:
The dark dock leaf
Spreads a tent
To hide your grief.
The thing you saw
In the forest pool
When you bent to drink
In the evening cool
Was a mask that He,
The Wisest Toad,
Gave us to hide
Our precious load—
The jewel that shines
In the flat toad-head
With gracious sapphire
And changing red.

For if, my toadling,
Your face were fair
As the precious jewel
That glimmers there,
Man, the jealous,
Man, the cruel,
Would look at you
And suspect the jewel.

So dry the tears
From your hornèd eyes,
And eat your supper
Of dew and flies;
Curl in the shade
Of the nettles deep,
Think of your jewel
And go to sleep.

STELLA GIBBONS

7. Snail

Snail upon the wall,
Have you got at all
Anything to tell
About your shell?

Only this, my child—
When the wind is wild,
Or when the sun is hot,
It's all I've got.

JOHN DRINKWATER

8. Heaven

Fish (fly-replete, in depth of June,
Dawdling away their wat'ry noon)
Ponder deep wisdom, dark or clear,
Each secret fishy hope or fear.
Fish say, they have their Stream and Pond;
But is there anything Beyond?
This life cannot be All, they swear,
For how unpleasant, if it were!
One may not doubt that, somehow, Good
Shall come of Water and of Mud;
And, sure, the reverent eye must see
A Purpose in Liquidity.
We darkly know, by Faith we cry,
The future is not Wholly Dry.
Mud unto mud!—Death eddies near—
Not here the appointed End, not here!
But somewhere, beyond Space and Time,
Is wetter water, slimier slime!
And there (they trust) there swimmeth One
Who swam ere rivers were begun,
Immense, of fishy form and mind,
Squamous, omnipotent and kind;
And under that Almighty Fin,
The littlest fish may enter in,
Oh! never fly conceals a hook,
Fish say, in the Eternal Brook,
But more than mundane weeds are there,
And mud, celestially fair;
Fat caterpillars drift around,
And Paradisal grubs are found;
Unfading moths, immortal flies,
And the worm that never dies.
And in that Heaven of all their wish,
There shall be no more land, say fish.

RUPERT BROOKE

9. The Giraffe

Hide of a leopard and hide of a deer
And eyes of a baby calf,
Sombre and large and crystal clear,
And a comical back that is almost sheer
Has the absurd giraffe.

A crane all covered with hide and hair
Is the aslant giraffe,
So cleverly mottled with many a square
That even the jungle is unaware
Whether a pair or a herd are there,
Or possibly one giraffe,
Or possibly only half.

If you saw him stoop and straddle and drink
He would certainly make you laugh,
He would certainly make you laugh, I think
With his head right down on the water's brink,
Would the invert giraffe,
The comical knock-kneed, angular, crock-kneed,
Anyhow-built giraffe.

There's more than a grain of common sense
And a husky lot of chaff
In the many and various arguments
About the first giraffe,
The first and worst giraffe;
Whether he grows a neck because
He yearned for the higher shoots
Out of the reach of all and each
Of the ruminating brutes;
Or whether he got to the shoots because
His neck was long, if long it was,
Is the cause of many disputes

Over the ladder without any rungs,
The stopper-like mouth and the longest of tongues
Of the rum and dumb giraffe,
The how-did-you-come giraffe,
The brown equatorial, semi-arboreal
Head-in-the-air giraffe.

GEOFFREY DEARMER

VI

BIRD SONGS

1. The Thrush's Nest

Within a thick and spreading hawthorn bush
  That overhung a mole-hill large and round,
I heard from morn to morn a merry thrush
  Sing hymns to sunrise, and I drank the sound
With joy; and, often an intruding guest,
  I watched her secret toils from day to day—
How true she warped the moss to form a nest,
  And modelled it within the wood and clay;
And by and by, like heath-bells gilt with dew,
  There lay her shining eggs, as bright as flowers,
Ink-spotted over shells of greeny blue;
  And there I witnessed, in the sunny hours,
A brood of nature's minstrels chirp and fly,
Glad as that sunshine and the laughing sky.

                  JOHN CLARE

2. The Nest

  Four blue stones in this thrush's nest
  I leave, content to make the best
  Of turquoise, lapis lazuli
  Or for that matter of the whole blue sky.

             ANDREW YOUNG

3. A Fragment

Repeat that, repeat,
Cuckoo, bird, and open ear wells, heart-springs, delightfully
  sweet,
With a ballad, with a ballad, a rebound
Off trundled timber and scoops of the hillside ground, hollow
  hollow hollow ground:
The whole landscape flushes on a sudden at a sound.

          GERARD MANLEY HOPKINS

4. The Ecstatic

Lark, skylark, spilling your rubbed and round
Pebbles of sound in air's still lake,
Whose widening circles fill the noon; yet none
Is known so small beside the sun:

Be strong your fervent soaring, your skyward air!
Tremble there, a nerve of song!
Float up there where voice and wing are one,
A singing star, a note of light!

Buoyed, embayed in heaven's noon-wide reaches—
For soon light's tide will turn—Oh stay!
Cease not till day streams to the west, then down
That estuary drop down to peace.

C. DAY LEWIS

5. A Minor Bird

I have wished a bird would fly away,
And not sing by my house all day;

Have clapped my hands at him from the door
When it seemed as if I could bear no more.

The fault must partly have been in me.
The bird was not to blame for his key.

And of course there must be something wrong
In wanting to silence any song.

ROBERT FROST

6. The Herons

As I was climbing Ardan Mor
From the shore of Sheelan lake,
I met the herons coming down
Before the waters wake.

And they were talking in their flight
Of dreamy ways the herons go
When all the hills are withered up
Nor any waters flow.

FRANCIS LEDWIDGE

7. *Humming-bird*

I can imagine, in some other world
Primeval-dumb, far back
In that most awful stillness, that only gasped and hummed,
Humming-birds raced down the avenues.

Before anything had a soul,
While life was a heave of Matter, half inanimate,
This little bit chipped off in brilliance
And went whizzing through the slow, vast, succulent stems.

I believe there were no flowers then,
In the world where the humming-bird flashed ahead of creation.
I believe he pierced the slow vegetable veins with his long beak.

Probably he was big
As mosses, and little lizards, they say, were once big.
Probably he was a jabbing, terrifying monster.

We look at him through the wrong end of the long telescope
of Time,
Luckily for us.

D. H. LAWRENCE

8. *The Owl*

When cats run home and light is come,
And dew is cold upon the ground,
And the far-off stream is dumb,
And the whirring sail goes round,
And the whirring sail goes round;
Alone and warming his five wits,
The white owl in the belfry sits.

When merry milkmaids click the latch,
　And rarely smells the new-mown hay,
And the cock hath sung beneath the thatch
　Twice or thrice his roundelay,
　Twice or thrice his roundelay;
　　Alone and warming his five wits,
　　The white owl in the belfry sits.

ALFRED, LORD TENNYSON

9. The Bird

As I went singing over the earth,
　Many a song I heard,—
A song of death and a song of mirth,
A song that was of little worth,
　And the song of a bird.

MARY COLERIDGE

VII

THE

HOMELY BEASTS

1. From *Two Songs of a Fool*

A speckled cat and a tame hare
Eat at my hearthstone
And sleep there;
And both look up to me alone
For learning and defence
As I look up to Providence.

I start out of my sleep to think
Some day I may forget
Their food and drink;
Or, the house door left unshut,
The hare may run till it's found
The horn's sweet note and the tooth of the hound.

I bear a burden that may well try
Men that do all by rule,
And what can I
That am a wandering-witted fool
But pray to God that He ease
My great responsibilities?

W. B. YEATS

2. From *The Task, The Winter Morning Walk*

Shaggy, and lean, and shrewd, with pointed ears
And tail cropp'd short, half lurcher and half cur—
His dog attends him. Close behind his heel
Now creeps he slow; and now, with many a frisk
Wide-scamp'ring, snatches up the drifted snow
With iv'ry teeth, or ploughs it with his snout;
Then shakes his powder'd coat, and barks for joy.

WILLIAM COWPER

3. To a Black Greyhound

Shining black in the shining light,
    Inky black in the golden sun,
Graceful as the swallow's flight,
    Light as swallow, wingèd one,
Swift as driven hurricane—
    Double-sinewed stretch and spring,
Muffled thud of flying feet,
    See the black dog galloping,
    Hear his wild foot-beat.

See him lie when the day is dead,
    Black curves curled on the boarded floor.
Sleepy eyes, my sleepy-head—
    Eyes that were aflame before.
Gentle now, they burn no more;
    Gentle now and softly warm,
With the fire that made them bright
    Hidden—as when after storm
    Softly falls the night.

God of speed, who makes the fire—
    God of Peace, who lulls the same—
God who gives the fierce desire,
    Lust for blood as fierce as flame—
God who stands in Pity's name—
    Many may ye be or less,
Ye who rule the earth and sun:
    Gods of strength and gentleness,
    Ye are ever one.

                JULIAN GRENFELL

4. Lone Dog

I'm a lean dog, a keen dog, a wild dog, and lone;
I'm a rough dog, a tough dog, hunting on my own;
I'm a bad dog, a mad dog, teasing silly sheep;
I love to sit and bay the moon, to keep fat souls from sleep.

I'll never be a lap dog, licking dirty feet,
A sleek dog, a meek dog, cringing for my meat;
Not for me the fireside, the well-filled plate,
But shut door, and sharp stone, and cuff, and kick, and hate.

Not for me the other dogs, running by my side;
Some have run a short while, but none of them would bide,
O mine is still the lone trail, the hard trail, the best,
Wide wind, and wild stars, and the hunger of the quest!

IRENE R. MCLEOD

5. *The Cat and the Moon*

The cat went here and there
The moon spun round like a top,
And the nearest kin of the moon,
The creeping cat, looked up.
Black Minnaloushe stared at the moon,
For, wander and wail as he would,
The pure cold light in the sky
Troubled his animal blood.
Minnaloushe runs in the grass
Lifting his delicate feet.
Do you dance, Minnaloushe, do you dance?
When two close kindred meet,
What better than call a dance?
Maybe the moon may learn,
Tired of that courtly fashion,
A new dance turn.
Minnaloushe creeps through the grass
From moonlit place to place,
The sacred moon overhead
Has taken a new phase.
Does Minnaloushe know that his pupils
Will pass from change to change,
And that from round to crescent,

From crescent to round they range?
Minnaloushe creeps through the grass
Alone, important and wise,
And lifts to the changing moon
His changing eyes.

W. B. YEATS

6. *Cats*

Cats, no less liquid than their shadows,
Offer no angles to the wind.
They slip, diminished, neat, through loopholes
Less than themselves; will not be pinned

To rules or routes for journeys; counter
Attack with non-resistance; twist
Enticing through the curving fingers
And leave an angered, empty fist.

They wait, obsequious as darkness,
Quick to retire, quick to return;
Admit no aims or ethics; flatter
With reservations; will not learn

To answer to their names; are seldom
Truly owned till shot and skinned.
Cats, no less liquid than their shadows,
Offer no angles to the wind.

A. S. J. TESSIMOND

7. *Macavity: the Mystery Cat*

Macavity's a Mystery Cat: he's called the Hidden Paw—
For he's the master criminal who can defy the Law.
He's the bafflement of Scotland Yard, the Flying Squad's
   despair:
For when they reach the scene of crime—*Macavity's not there!*

Macavity, Macavity, there's no one like Macavity,
He's broken every human law, he breaks the law of gravity.
His powers of levitation would make a fakir stare,
And when you reach the scene of crime—*Macavity's not there!*
You may seek him in the basement, you may look up in the
air—
But I tell you once and once again, *Macavity's not there!*

Macavity's a ginger cat, he's very tall and thin;
You would know him if you saw him, for his eyes are sunken in.
His brow is deeply lined with thought, his head is highly
domed;
His coat is dusty from neglect, his whiskers are uncombed.
He sways his head from side to side, with movements like a
snake;
And when you think he's half asleep, he's always wide awake.

Macavity, Macavity, there's no one like Macavity,
For he's a fiend in feline shape, a monster of depravity.
You may meet him in a by-street, you may see him in the
square—
But when a crime's discovered, then *Macavity's not there!*

He's outwardly respectable. (They say he cheats at cards.)
And his footprints are not found in any file of Scotland Yard's.
And when the larder's looted, or the jewel-case is rifled,
Or when the milk is missing, or another Peke's been stifled,
Or the greenhouse glass is broken, and the trellis past repair—
Ay, there's the wonder of the thing! *Macavity's not there!*

And when the Foreign Office find a Treaty's gone astray,
Or the Admiralty lose some plans and drawings by the way,
There may be a scrap of paper in the hall or on the stair—
But it's useless to investigate—*Macavity's not there!*
And when the loss has been disclosed, the Secret Service say:
'It must have been Macavity!'—but he's a mile away.
You'll be sure to find him resting, or a-licking of his thumbs,
Or engaged in doing complicated long division sums.

Macavity, Macavity, there's no one like Macavity,
There never was a Cat of such deceitfulness and suavity.
He always has an alibi, and one or two to spare:
At whatever time the deed took place—MACAVITY
WASN'T THERE!
And they say that all the cats whose wicked deeds are widely
known
(I might mention Mungojerrie, I might mention Griddlebone)
Are nothing more than agents for the Cat who all the time
Just controls their operations: the Napoleon of Crime!

T. S. ELIOT

8. The Cat

Hark! She is calling to her cat.
She is down the misty garden in a tatter-brim straw hat,
And broken slippers grass-wet, treading tearful daisies.
But he does not heed her. He sits still—and gazes.

Where the laden gooseberry leans over to the rose,
He sits thorn-protected, gazing down his nose.
Coffee-coloured skies above him press upon the sun;
Bats about his mistress flitter-flutter one by one;

Jessamines drop perfume; the nightingales begin;
Nightjars wind their humdrum notes; a crescent moon rides
thin;
The daybird chorus dies away, the air shrinks chill and grey.
Her lonely voice still calls him—but her panther won't come in!

RICHARD CHURCH

VIII

HORSES AND RIDERS

1. *Horses*

'Newmarket or St Leger'

Who, in the garden-pony carrying skeps
Of grass or fallen leaves, his knees gone slack,
Round belly, hollow back,
Sees the Mongolian Tarpan of the Steppes?
Or, in the Shire with plaits and feathered feet,
The war-horse like the wind the Tartar knew?
Or, in the Suffolk Punch, spells out anew
The wild grey asses fleet
With stripe from head to tail, and moderate ears?
In cross sea-donkeys, sheltering as storm gathers,
The mountain zebras maned upon the withers,
With round enormous ears?

And who in thoroughbreds in stable garb
Of blazoned rug, ranged orderly, will mark
The wistful eyelashes so long and dark,
And call to mind the old blood of the Barb?
And that slim island on whose bare campaigns
Galloped with flying manes,
For a king's pleasure, churning surf and scud,
A white Arabian stud?

That stallion, teazer to Hobgoblin, free
And foaled upon a plain of Barbary:
Godolphin Barb, who dragged a cart for hire
In Paris, but became a famous sire,
Covering all lovely mares, and she who threw
Rataplan to the Baron, loveliest shrew;
King Charles's royal mares; the Dodsworth Dam;
And the descendants: Yellow Turk, King Tom;
And Lath out of Roxana, famous foal;
Careless; Eclipse, unbeaten in the race,
With white blaze on his face;
Prunella who was dam to Parasol.

Blood Arab, pony, pedigree, no name,
All horses are the same:
The Shetland stallion stunted by the damp,
Yet filled with self-importance, stout and small;
The Cleveland slow and tall;
New Forests that may ramp
Their lives out, being branded, breeding free
When bluebells turn the Forest to a sea,
When mares with foals at foot flee down the glades,
Sheltering in bramble coverts
From mobs of corn-fed lovers;
Or, at the acorn harvest, in stockades
A round-up being afoot, will stand at bay,
Or, making for the heather clearings, splay
Wide-spread towards the bogs by gorse and whin,
Roped as they flounder in
By foresters.

       But hunters as day fails
Will take the short-cut home across the fields;
With slackened rein will stoop through darkening wealds;
With creaking leathers skirt the swedes and kales;
Patient, adventuring still,
A horse's ears bob on the distant hill;
He starts to hear
A pheasant chuck or whirr, having the fear
In him of ages filled with war and raid,
Night gallop, ambuscade;
Remembering adventures of his kin
With giant winged worms that coiled round mountain bases,
And Nordic tales of young gods riding races
Up courses of the rainbow; here, within
The depth of Hampshire hedges, does he dream
How Athens woke, to hear above her roofs
The welkin flash and thunder to the hoofs
Of Dawn's tremendous team?

DOROTHY WELLESLEY

2. Duchess

The trace-horse, watch her move;
She takes the hill as a ship,
Figure-head noble,
Devours the steepening wave.
Forehead of midnight caught
In a brass net she coins the light;
Might sleeked with sweat,
A shoulder firm as marble;
Watch her, the great feet grip
Our ground-swell earth, all's set
For home now, tackle taut;
She leans to the work soberly, with love.

Earth dimmed, she wears the dark;
The last load brushing a star
Rocks into haven,
Sheds whispering in its wake
Lavender leavings, rich moon-catch
Too rare to touch;
Glint hands unhitch
Moth horses silverly graven.
Look at her, gloaming fur
Rope-rough she roams, a witch;
Yonder what cobweb leech
Is milking the pond stealthily of black.

The stark days, soon they come;
An old mare under the hedge,
Rump to the blizzard,
Is carved on the year's tomb.
Wind-bitten Duchess, breast
Frost-laced she glows august,
Knows winter's worst,
Lean havoc, storm-shock hazard.

Leave her to rust, nor grudge
This yoke-proud labourer lost;
Scored flank December-fleeced
She conjures the snow softly into bloom.

LILIAN BOWES LYON

3. *The Runaway*

Once when the snow of the year was beginning to fall,
We stopped by a mountain pasture to say, 'Whose colt?'
A little Morgan had one forefoot on the wall,
The other curled at his breast. He dipped his head
And snorted at us. And then he had to bolt.
We heard the miniature thunder where he fled,
And we saw him, or thought we saw him, dim and grey,
Like a shadow against the curtain of falling flakes.
'I think the little fellow's afraid of the snow.
He isn't winter-broken. It isn't play
With the little fellow at all. He's running away.
I doubt if even his mother could tell him, "Sakes,
It's only weather." He'd think she didn't know!
Where is his mother? He can't be out alone.'
And now he comes again with clatter of stone,
And mounts the wall again with whited eyes
And all his tail that isn't hair up straight.
He shudders his coat as if to throw off flies.
'Whoever it is that leaves him out so late,
When other creatures have gone to stall and bin,
Ought to be told to come and take him in.'

ROBERT FROST

4. *Horses*

Those lumbering horses in the steady plough,
On the bare field—I wonder why, just now,
They seemed so terrible, so wild and strange,
Like magic power on the stony grange.

186

Perhaps some childish hour has come again,
When I watched fearful, through the blackening rain,
Their hooves like pistons in an ancient mill
Move up and down, yet seem as standing still.

Their conquering hooves which trod the stubble down
Were ritual which turned the field to brown,
And their great hulks were seraphim of gold,
Or mute ecstatic monsters on the mould.

And oh the rapture, when, one furrow done,
They marched broad-breasted to the sinking sun!
The light flowed off their bossy sides in flakes;
The furrows rolled behind like struggling snakes.

But when at dusk with steaming nostrils home
They came, they seemed gigantic in the gloam,
And warm and glowing with mysterious fire,
Which lit their smouldering bodies in the mire.

Their eyes as brilliant and as wide as night
Gleamed with a cruel apocalyptic light.
Their manes the leaping ire of the wind
Lifted with rage invisible and blind.

Ah, now it fades! it fades! and I must pine
Again for that dread country crystalline,
Where the blank fields and the still-standing tree
Were bright and fearful presences to me.

EDWIN MUIR

5. The Winged Horse

It's ten years ago today you turned me out o' doors
To cut my feet on flinty lands and stumble down the shores,
And I thought about the all-in-all, oh more than I can tell!
And I caught a horse to ride upon and I rode him very well,
He had flame behind the eyes of him and wings upon his side.
    And I ride, and I ride!

187

I rode him out of Wantage and I rode him up the hill,
And there I saw the Beacon in the morning standing still,
Inkpen and Hackpen and southward away
High through the middle airs in the strengthening of the day,
And there I saw the channel-glint and England in her pride.
     And I ride, and I ride!

And once a-top of Lambourne down toward the hill of Clere
I saw the Host of Heaven in rank and Michael with his spear,
And Turpin out of Gascony and Charlemagne the Lord,
And Roland of the marches with his hand upon his sword
For the time he should have need of it, and forty more beside.
     And I ride, and I ride!

For you that took the all-in-all the things you left were three.
A loud voice for singing and keen eyes to see,
And a spouting well of joy within that never yet was dried!
     And I ride.

HILAIRE BELLOC

6. *Mirage*

I saw a man on a horse
Riding against the sun.
'Hallo! Don Cossack!' I cried.
He shouted 'Hallo, my son!'

The Caspian Sea shimmered;
The Kazac tents shone
For a moment in England,
Then the horseman was gone.

RICHARD CHURCH

188

7. *After Passing the Examination*

For ten years I never left my books;
I went up . . . and won unmerited praise.
My high place I do not much prize;
The joy of my parents will first make me proud.
Fellow students, six or seven men,
See me off as I leave the City gate.
My covered coach is ready to drive away;
Flutes and strings blend their parting tune.
Hopes achieved dull the pains of parting;
Fumes of wine shorten the long road. . .
Shod with wings is the horse of him who rides
On a Spring day the road that leads to home.

PO CHU-I (A.D. 772–846)
Translated by ARTHUR WALEY

8. *Together*

Splashing along the boggy woods all day,
And over brambled hedge and holding clay,
I shall not think of him:
But when the watery fields grow brown and dim,
And hounds have lost their fox, and horses tire,
I know that he'll be with me on my way
Home through the darkness to the evening fire.

He's jumped each stile along the glistening lanes;
His hand will be upon the mud-soaked reins;
Hearing the saddle creak,
He'll wonder if the frost will come next week.
I shall forget him in the morning light;
And while we gallop on he will not speak:
But at the stable-door he'll say good-night.

SIEGFRIED SASSOON

9. *Windy Nights*

Whenever the moon and stars are set,
    Whenever the wind is high,
All night long in the dark and wet,
    A man goes riding by.
Late in the night when the fires are out,
Why does he gallop and gallop about?

Whenever the trees are crying aloud,
    And ships are tossed at sea,
By, on the highway, low and loud,
    By at the gallop goes he.
By at the gallop he goes, and then
By he comes back at the gallop again.

ROBERT LOUIS STEVENSON

1
WONDER

1. *Tell me, Tell me, Smiling Child*

Tell me, tell me, smiling child,
What the past is like to thee?
'An Autumn evening soft and mild,
With a wind that sighs mournfully.'

Tell me, what is the present hour?
'A green and flowery spray,
Where a young bird sits gathering its power
To mount and fly away.'

And what is the future, happy one?
'A sea beneath a cloudless sun;
A mighty, glorious, dazzling sea
Stretching into infinity.'

EMILY BRONTË

2. *The World*

When Adam first did from his dust arise;
    He did not see,
    Nor could there be
A greater joy before his eyes:
The sun as bright for me doth shine;
    The spheres above
    Did show his love,
While they to kiss the earth incline,
The stars as great a service do;
    The moon as much I view
As Adam did, and all God's works divine
    Are glorious still, and mine.

Sin spoil'd them; but my Saviour's precious blood
    Sprinkled I see
    On them to be,
Making them all both safe and good:

With greater rapture I admire
That I from hell
Redeem'd, do dwell
On earth as yet; and here a fire
Not scorching but refreshing glows,
And living water flows,
Which Dives more than silver doth request,
Of crystals far the best.

What shall I render unto Thee, my God,
For teaching me
The wealth to see
Which doth enrich Thy great abode?
My virgin-thoughts in childhood were
Full of content,
And innocent,
Without disturbance, free and clear,
Ev'n like the streams of crystal springs.
Where all the curious things
Do from the bottom of the well appear
When no filth or mud is there.

For so when first I in the summer fields
Saw golden corn
The earth adorn,
(This day that sight its pleasure yields)
No rubies could more take mine eye;
Nor pearls of price,
By man's device
In gold set artificially,
Could of more worth appear to me,
How rich so'er they be
By men esteem'd; nor could these more be mine
That on my finger shine.

The azure skies did with so sweet a smile,
       Their curtains spread
       Above my head
And with its height mine eye beguile;
So lovely did the distant green
       That fring'd the field
       Appear, and yield
Such pleasant prospects to be seen
From neighb'ring hills; no precious stone,
       Or crown, or royal throne,
Which do bedeck the richest Indian lord,
       Could such delight afford.

The sun, that gilded all the bordering woods,
       Shone from the sky
       To beautify
My earthly and my heavenly goods;
Exalted in his throne on high,
       He shed his beams
       In golden streams
That did illustrate all the sky;
Those floods of light, his nimble rays,
       Did fill the glitt'ring ways,
While that unsufferable piercing eye
       That ground did glorify.

The choicest colours, yellow, green, and blue
       Did all this court
       In comely sort
With mixt varieties bestrew;
Like gold with emeralds between;
       As if my God
       From His abode
By these intended to be seen.
And so He was: I Him descry'd
       In's works, the surest Guide
Dame nature yields; His love, His life doth there
       For evermore appear.

No house nor holder in this world did I
        Observe to be;
        What I did see
Seem'd all mine own; wherein did lie
A mine, a garden, of delights;
        Pearls were but stones;
        And great king's thrones,
Compared with such benefits,
But empty chairs; a crown, a toy
        Scarce apt to please a boy.
All other are but petty trifling shows,
        To that which God bestows.

A Royal Crown, inlaid with precious stones,
        Did less surprise
        The infant-eyes
Of many other little ones,
Than the great beauties of this frame,
        Made for my sake
        Mine eyes did take,
Which I divine, and mine, do name.
Surprising joys beyond all price
        Compos'd a Paradise,
Which did my soul to love my God enflame,
        And ever doth the same.

THOMAS TRAHERNE

3. From *Man's Mortality*

Like as the damask rose you see,
Or like the blossom on the tree,
Or like the dainty flower of May,
Or like the morning of the day,
Or like the sun, or like the shade,
Or like the gourd which Jonas had:
Even such is Man; whose thread is spun,
Drawn out, and cut, and so is done.

The rose withers, the blossom blasteth,
The flower fades, the morning hasteth:
The sun sets, the shadow flies;
The gourd consumes, and man he dies.

Like to the grass that's newly sprung,
Or like a tale that's new begun:
Or like the bird that's here today,
Or like the pearled dew of May;
Or like an hour, or like a span,
Or like the singing of a swan:
Even such is Man, who lives by breath;
Is here, now there: so life, and death.
The grass withers, the tale is ended,
The bird is flown, the dew's ascended,
The hour is short, the span not long;
The swan's near death; Man's life is done.

Like to the bubble in the brook,
Or in a glass much like a look,
Or like a shuttle in weaver's hand,
Or like a writing on the sand,
Or like a thought, or like a dream,
Or like the gliding of the stream:
Even such is Man, who lives by breath;
Is here, now there: so life, and death.
The bubble's cut, the look's forgot,
The shuttle's flung, the writing's blot,
The thought is past, the dream is gone;
The water glides; Man's life is done.

Like to an arrow from the bow,
Or like swift course of watery flow,
Or like the time 'twixt flood and ebb,
Or like the spider's tender web,
Or like a race, or like a goal,
Or like the dealing of a dole:
Even such is Man, whose brittle state
Is always subject unto Fate.

The arrow's shot, the flood soon spent,
The time no time, the web soon rent,
The race soon run, the goal soon won,
The dole soon dealt, Man's life first done.

Like to the lightning from the sky,
Or like a post that quick doth hie,
Or like a quaver in short song,
Or like a journey three days long,
Or like the snow when summer's come,
Or like the pear, or like the plum:
Even such is man, who heaps up sorrow,
Lives but this day and dies tomorrow.
The lightning's past, the post must go,
The song is short, the journey's so,
The pear doth rot, the plum doth fall,
The snow dissolves, and so must all.

ANON

4. *Dartside*

I cannot tell what you say, green leaves,
     I cannot tell what you say:
But I know that there is a spirit in you,
     And a word in you this day.

I cannot tell what you say, rosy rocks,
     I cannot tell what you say:
But I know that there is a spirit in you,
     And a word in you this day.

I cannot tell what you say, brown streams,
     I cannot tell what you say:
But I know that in you too a spirit doth live,
     And a word doth speak this day.

'Oh green is the colour of faith and truth,
And rose the colour of love and youth,
   And brown of the fruitful clay.
Sweet Earth is faithful, and fruitful, and young,
And her bridal day shall come ere long,
And you shall know what the rocks and the streams
   And the whispering woodlands say.'

CHARLES KINGSLEY

5. The Roaring Frost

A flock of winds came winging from the North,
Strong birds with fighting pinions driving forth
   With a resounding call:—

Where will they close their wings and cease their cries—
Between what warming seas and conquering skies—
   And fold, and fall?

ALICE MEYNELL

6. Nothing is Enough

Nothing is enough!
No, though our all be spent—
Heart's extremest love,
Spirit's whole intent,
All that nerve can feel,
All that brain invent,—
Still beyond appeal
Will Divine Desire
Yet more excellent
Precious cost require
Of this mortal stuff,—
Never be content
Till ourselves be fire.
Nothing is enough!

LAURENCE BINYON

7. *Dear Perfection*

In the least flowering weed she lies,
Those buds are eyes,
Those leaves are hands, that little stem
Body and arms that flourish them;
That seed's a crown;
Those dews are tears that tremble down.

That look is hers, the attitude,
The solitude:
The dear simplicity suffices,
Shaming the sum of my devices;
See how she prays,
Speaketh, and sings in divers ways.

Sometimes I see her smile in men;
The impotent pen
Craves to be broken, and the mind
Never the noble word can find
To sing their state
Or their most worth to celebrate.

I can but say that I have seen
Her beauty clean
Shine in the humble, and her grace
Look from simplicity's own face:
Then do I smile
And sigh for very love the while.

There is a place where she must be
A deity:
There on a day she'll bid me tell
These that I loved them very well;
But now I keep
Silence, and bid my love go sleep.

But here's where she is wholly mine:
Up from the line
Of lovely verse she leaps, and takes
In her strong hand my soul that shakes,
That faints and dies,
Yet lives by looking in her eyes.

Dearest Perfection! let me be
A spark of thee;
Light my small taper at thy fire
And live a flame of pure desire:
Shine like the sun,
Burn like the Phoenix, which is one.

RUTH PITTER

8. *A Song About Myself*

From a letter to Fanny Keats

There was a naughty Boy,
    And a naughty Boy was he,
He ran away to Scotland
    The people for to see—
        There he found
        That the ground
        Was as hard,
        That a yard
        Was as long,
        That a song
        Was as merry,
        That a cherry
        Was as red—
        That lead
        Was as weighty,
        That fourscore
        Was as eighty,
        That a door
        Was as wooden
        As in England—

So he stood in
    His shoes and he wonder'd,
    He wonder'd,
He stood in his
    Shoes and he wonder'd.

JOHN KEATS

II

ALL THINGS LOVELY

1. *Pied Beauty*

Glory be to God for dappled things—
    For skies of couple-colour as a brinded cow;
        For rose-moles all in stipple upon trout that swim;
Fresh fire-coal chestnut-falls; finches' wings;
    Landscape plotted and pieced—fold, fallow, and plough;
        And all trades, their gear and tackle and trim.

All things counter, original, spare, strange;
    Whatever is fickle, freckled (who knows how?)
        With swift, slow; sweet, sour; adazzle, dim;
He fathers-forth whose beauty is past change:
           Praise Him.

               GERARD MANLEY HOPKINS

2. From *A Song to David*

Strong is the horse upon his speed;
Strong in pursuit the rapid glede,
    Which makes at once his game:
Strong the tall ostrich on the ground;
Strong through the turbulent profound
    Shoots xiphias[1] to his aim.

Strong is the lion—like a coal
His eye-ball—like a bastion's mole
    His chest against the foes:
Strong, the gier-eagle on his sail,
Strong against tide, th' enormous whale
    Emerges as he goes.

But stronger still, in earth and air,
And in the sea, the man of pray'r,
    And far beneath the tide;
And in the seat to faith assign'd,
Where ask is have, where seek is find,
    Where knock is open wide.

        [1] The sword-fish.

Beauteous the fleet before the gale;
Beauteous the multitudes in mail,
    Rank'd arms and crested heads:
Beauteous the garden's umbrage mild,
Walk, water, meditated wild,
    And all the bloomy beds.

.   .   .   .   .   .

Beauteous, yea beauteous more than these,
The shepherd king upon his knees,
    For his momentous trust;
With wish of infinite conceit,
For man, beast, mute, the small and great,
    And prostrate dust to dust.

.   .   .   .   .   .

Glorious the sun in mid career;
Glorious th' assembled fires appear;
    Glorious the comet's train:
Glorious the trumpet and alarm;
Glorious th' almighty stretch'd-out arm;
    Glorious th' enraptured main:

Glorious the northern lights astream;
Glorious the song, when God's the theme
    Glorious the thunder's roar:
Glorious hosanna from the den;
Glorious the catholic amen;
    Glorious the martyr's gore:

Glorious—more glorious is the crown
Of Him that brought salvation down
    By meekness, call'd thy Son;
Thou that stupendous truth believ'd,
And now the matchless deed's achiev'd,
    DETERMINED, DARED, and DONE.

CHRISTOPHER SMART

3. Bewitched

Give me a night in June that's clear and quiet,
    That I may stare at Heaven until I see
Her face all twitching to her farthest star—
    Conscious of one true man's idolatry.

I stare at dewdrops till they close their eyes,
    I stare at grass till all the world is green;
I stare at rainbows all their precious life,
    Till nothing's left to prove what I have seen.

I stare at Robin Redbreast on his bough,
    Till he comes down with many a pretty dance:
I stare at my own Self, and walk the earth
    With half my spirit in a wonder-trance.

W. H. DAVIES

4. In the Fields

Lord, when I look at lovely things which pass,
    Under old trees the shadows of young leaves
Dancing to please the wind along the grass,
    Or the gold stillness of the August sun on the August
      sheaves;
Can I believe that there is a heavenlier world than this?
    And if there is
Will the strange heart of any everlasting thing
    Bring me these dreams that take my breath away?
They come at evening with the home-flying rooks and the
      scent of hay,
    Over the fields. They come in Spring.

CHARLOTTE MEW

5. *An Emerald is as Green as Grass*

An emerald is as green as grass;
　A ruby red as blood;
A sapphire shines as blue as heaven;
　A flint lies in the mud.

A diamond is a brilliant stone,
　To catch the world's desire;
An opal holds a fiery spark;
　But a flint holds fire.

CHRISTINA ROSSETTI

6. *How Happy is the Little Stone*

How happy is the little stone
That rambles in the road alone,
And doesn't care about careers,
And exigencies never fears;
Whose coat of elemental brown
A passing universe put on;
And independent as the sun,
Associates or glows alone,
Fulfilling absolute decree
In casual simplicity.

EMILY DICKINSON

7. *Music*

When music sounds, gone is the earth I know,
And all her lovely things even lovelier grow;
Her flowers in vision flame, her forest trees
Lift burdened branches, stilled with ecstasies.

When music sounds, out of the water rise
Naiads whose beauty dims my waking eyes,
Rapt in strange dreams burns each enchanted face,
With solemn echoing stirs their dwelling-place.

When music sounds, all that I was I am
Ere to this haunt of brooding dust I came;
While from Time's woods break into distant song
The swift-winged hours, as I hasten along.

WALTER DE LA MARE

8. All Sounds Have Been as Music
(A fragment)

All sounds have been as music to my listening:
    Pacific lamentations of slow bells,
The crunch of boots on blue snow rosy-glistening,
    Shuffle of autumn leaves; and all farewells:

Bugles that sadden all the evening air,
    And country bells clamouring their last appeals
Before [the] music of the evening prayer;
    Bridges, sonorous under carriage wheels.

Gurgle of sluicing surge through hollow rocks,
    The gluttonous lapping of the waves on weeds,
Whisper of grasses; the myriad-tinkling flocks,
    The warbling drawl of flutes and shepherds' reeds.

Thrilling of throstles in the clear blue dawn,
    Bees fumbling and fuming over sainfoin-fields.

WILFRED OWEN

9. Gifts

Tell me no more that I am one
Who still takes all things, to give naught;
For, if you say so, you betray
    A friendship bought.

I would not bring you, if I could,
Venetian silks of gold and red,
Nor carve from delicate ivory
    Crowns for your head.

No turquoise casket would I give,
Laden with spice from Samarcand,
No cedarwood, no pale sea pearl
    To grace your hand.

Brocades will rot and perfumes fade,
Rare, lustrous metals dull with rust,
And what in us is fair as they
    Must fall to dust.

No; I would rather shake and rouse
Those sluggish senses, that your mind
Might fly with a swallow south, and take
    Gifts from the wind,

And gifts from April, when her fields
With daisies foam the grassy seas
That wash about the rocky roots
    Of poplar-trees.

For if our souls drink beauty up
From wind and flower, from cloud and sun,
We'll keep some fragmentary grace
    When this world's done.

VIOLA GERARD GARVIN

10. *A Great Time*

Sweet Chance, that led my steps abroad,
    Beyond the town, where wild flowers grow—
A rainbow and a cuckoo, Lord,
    How rich and great the times are now!

Know, all ye sheep
And cows, that keep
On staring that I stand so long
In grass that's wet from heavy rain—
A rainbow and a cuckoo's song
May never come together again;
May never come
This side the tomb.

W. H. DAVIES

III

THE SINGING
WILL NEVER BE DONE

1. *Sung in Spring*

The gorse is on the granite,
    The light is growing clear,
Our tilted tacking planet
    Has another course to steer:
Without a wind to fill her
    She can hold upon the tack.
The Captain's lashed the tiller
    So we dance upon the deck.

Some ships go by a motor,
    And some by sails and spars,
But our ship is a rotor
    And she rolls among the stars
And has no fear of crashing:
    Without a spyglass even
You can see the signals flashing
    From the light-houses of Heaven.

Our vessel in her sailing
    Just nods and bowls along,
And half her crew are ailing
    And half are growing strong;
And some make strange grimaces
    At us who dance and shout:
The news from outer spaces
    Depends on who looks out.

Some ships by island spices
    Are scented as they run
Or through ice precipices
    Behold the midnight sun;
And these go home to haven
    For they are trading ships,
But we are touring Heaven
    And we tour in an ellipse.

We do not fear commotions
        Or anything untoward
From rocks or winds or oceans,
        We have them all on board
With sea-room all prevailing
        For a never-ending trip;
Was there ever such a sailing?
        Was there ever such a ship?

We have not once been harboured
        Since first we left the slips;
We see to port and starboard
        Brave bright companion ships,
And they go with us roundly;
        But we in hammocks rocked
Shall be sleeping very soundly
        Before our ship is docked.

She leaves no wake behind her,
        No foam before her foot
Because the gods designed her
        A rainbow-rolling boat.
We only know she's rolling
        And all the more we sing
Because just now we're bowling
        And rolling into Spring.

No questions can prevail on
        The Master of the Ship;
He won't say why we sail on
        This never-ending trip:
Though young and old and ailing
        Hold contradictory views
I think that simply sailing
        Is the meaning of the cruise.

OLIVER ST JOHN GOGARTY

2. *Sing me a Song of a Lad that is gone*

Sing me a song of a lad that is gone,
    Say, could that lad be I?
Merry of soul he sailed on a day
    Over the sea to Skye.

Mull was astern, Rum on the port,
    Eigg on the starboard bow;
Glory of youth glowed in his soul:
    Where is that glory now?

Sing me a song of a lad that is gone,
    Say, could that lad be I?
Merry of soul he sailed on a day
    Over the sea to Skye.

Give me again all that was there,
    Give me the sun that shone!
Give me the eyes, give me the soul,
    Give me the lad that's gone!

Sing me a song of a lad that is gone,
    Say, could that lad be I?
Merry of soul he sailed on a day
    Over the sea to Skye.

Billow and breeze, islands and seas,
    Mountains of rain and sun,
All that was good, all that was fair,
    All that was me is gone.

ROBERT LOUIS STEVENSON

3. *Madly Singing in the Mountains*

There is no one among men who has not a special failing:
And my failing consists in writing verses.
I have broken away from the thousand ties of life:
But this infirmity still remains behind.

213

Each time that I look at a fine landscape:
Each time that I meet a loved friend,
I raise my voice and recite a stanza of poetry
And am glad as though a God had crossed my path.
Ever since the day I was banished to Hsün-yang
Half my time I have lived among the hills.
And often, when I have finished a new poem,
Alone I climb the road to the Eastern Rock.
I lean my body on the banks of white Stone:
I pull down with my hands a green cassia branch.
My mad singing startles the valleys and the hills:
The apes and the birds all come to peep.
Fearing to become a laughing-stock to the world,
I choose a place that is unfrequented by men.

PO CHÜ-I
Translated by ARTHUR WALEY

4. *Everyone Sang*

Everyone suddenly burst out singing;
And I was filled with such delight
As prisoned birds must find in freedom
Winging wildly across the white
Orchards and dark green fields; on; on; and out of sight.

Everyone's voice was suddenly lifted,
And beauty came like the setting sun.
My heart was shaken with tears, and horror
Drifted away. . . . O but everyone
Was a bird; and the song was wordless; the singing will never
be done.

SIEGFRIED SASSOON

5. *The Song of the Children*

The World is ours till sunset,
Holly and fire and snow;
And the name of our dead brother
Who loved us long ago.

The grown folk mighty and cunning,
  They write his name in gold;
But we can tell a little
  Of the million tales he told.

He taught them laws and watchwords,
  To preach and struggle and pray;
But he taught us deep in the hayfield
  The games that the angels play.

Had he stayed here for ever,
  Their world would be wise as ours—
And the king be cutting capers
  And the priest be picking flowers.

But the dark day came: they gathered:
  On their faces we could see
They had taken and slain our brother,
  And hanged him on a tree.

                          G. K. CHESTERTON

6. So, We'll Go no More a Roving

So, we'll go no more a roving
  So late into the night,
Though the heart be still as loving,
  And the moon be still as bright.

For the sword outwears its sheath,
  And the soul wears out the breast,
And the heart must pause to breathe,
  And love itself have rest.

Though the night was made for loving,
  And the day returns too soon,
Yet we'll go no more a roving
  By the light of the moon.

                              LORD BYRON

7. Song from *The Princess*

The splendour falls on castle walls
    And snowy summits old in story:
The long light shakes across the lakes,
    And the wild cataract leaps in glory.
Blow, bugle, blow, set the wild echoes flying,
Blow, bugle; answer, echoes, dying, dying, dying.

O hark, O hear! how thin and clear,
    And thinner, clearer, farther going!
O sweet and far from cliff and scar
    The horns of Elfland faintly blowing!
Blow, let us hear the purple glens replying:
Blow bugle; answer, echoes, dying, dying, dying.

O love, they die in yon rich sky,
    They faint on hill or field or river:
Our echoes roll from soul to soul,
    And grow for ever and for ever.
Blow, bugle, blow, set the wild echoes flying,
And answer, echoes, answer, dying, dying, dying.

ALFRED, LORD TENNYSON

8. *Deer and Bracken*

The car stopped at the wood's edge.
We watched the freckled deer
Eating the pale green fronds.
All England's past was here.

Since first her wooded humps began
To form the green hills we know,
Men have watched the deer
Browse in her flowers and snow.

And I dreamed of England robbed of power,
Her roads moss-sunk, her towns fern-blind,
And wandering in her heart
A stag, a fawn and a hind.

For somewhere England's heart is hidden.
Its image haunts her lanes by day
And my dreams by night. The deer know
(If aught may know) the way.

If England could lose her Eastern rubies,
And Afric metals fierce,
And sunk into slumber
Only the deer's roar could pierce,

And her sons could rest within her heart,
Hearing a happy singing go
Up from her hidden poets
In months of flowers and snow . . .

Silent, we watched the deer.
The ghost-does glided in evening air
While the bucks fed in the shadowed fern.
All England's song was there.

STELLA GIBBONS

9. Song from *Mirage*

*(Sung to a guitar by 'a young favourite Kurd, a mongrel child of the
bazaar, whose voice was like a singing bird')*

I know a Room where tulips tall
   And almond-blossom pale
Are coloured on the frescoed wall.

I know a River where the ships
   Drift by with ghostly sail
And dead men chant with merry lips.

I know the Garden by the sea
   Where birds with painted wings
Mottle the dark magnolia Tree.

I know the never-failing Source,
   I know the Bush that sings,
The Vale of Gems, the flying Horse,

I know the Dog that was a Prince,
　　　The talking Nightingale,
The Hill of glass, the magic Quince,

I know the lovely Lake of Van;
　　　Yet, knowing all these things,
　　　I wander with a caravan,
　　　I wander with a caravan!

V. SACKVILLE-WEST

IV
PLAY AND PUZZLE

1. Song

The merry waves dance up and down, and play,
    Sport is granted to the sea.
Birds are the queristers of the empty air,
    Sport is never wanting there.
The ground doth smile at the spring's flowery birth,
    Sport is granted to the earth.
The fire its cheering flame on high doth rear,
    Sport is never wanting there.
If all the elements, the earth, the sea,
    Air, and fire, so merry be;
Why is man's mirth so seldom, and so small,
    Who is compounded of them all?

ABRAHAM COWLEY

2. The Dancing Cabman

Alone on the lawn
    The cabman dances;
In the dew of the dawn
    He kicks and prances.
His bowler is set
    On his bullet-head.
For his boots are wet
    And his aunt is dead.
There on the lawn
    As the light advances,
On the tide of the dawn,
    The cabman dances.

Swift and strong
    As a garden roller,
He dances along
    In his little bowler,

Skimming the lawn
    With royal grace,
The dew of the dawn
    On his great red face.
To fairy flutes,
    As the light advances,
In square, black boots
    The cabman dances.

J. B. MORTON

3. Jabberwocky

'Twas brillig, and the slithy toves
    Did gyre and gimble in the wabe:
All mimsy were the borogoves,
    And the mome raths outgrabe.

'Beware the Jabberwock, my son!
    The jaws that bite, the claws that catch!
Beware the Jubjub bird, and shun
    The frumious Bandersnatch!'

He took his vorpal sword in hand:
    Long time the manxome foe he sought—
So rested he by the Tumtum tree,
    And stood awhile in thought.

And, as in uffish thought he stood,
    The Jabberwock, with eyes of flame,
Came whiffling through the tulgey wood,
    And burbled as it came!

One, two! One, two! And through and through
    The vorpal blade went snicker-snack!
He left it dead, and with its head
    He went galumphing back.

'And hast thou slain the Jabberwock?
          Come to my arms, my beamish boy!
O frabjous day! Callooh! Callay!'
          He chortled in his joy.

'Twas brillig, and the slithy toves
          Did gyre and gimble in the wabe:
All mimsy were the borogoves,
          And the mome raths outgrabe.

                              LEWIS CARROLL

4. *The Hen and the Carp*

Once, in a roostery
there lived a speckled hen, and whenever she laid an egg this hen
     ecstatically cried:
'O progeny miraculous, particular spectaculous,
     what a wonderful hen am I!'

Down in a pond nearby
perchance a fat and broody carp
was basking, but her ears were sharp—
     she heard Dame Cackle cry:
'O progeny miraculous, particular spectaculous,
     what a wonderful hen am I!'

'Ah, Cackle,' bubbled she,
'for your single egg, O silly one,
I lay at least a million;
     suppose for each I cried:
"O progeny miraculous, particular spectaculous!"
     what a hullaballoo there'd be!'

                         IAN SERRAILLIER

222

5. *If*

If all the world were paper,
And all the sea were ink,
If all the trees were bread and cheese,
How should we do for drink?

If all the world were sand'o,
Oh then what should we lack'o;
If as they say there were no clay;
How should we take tobacco?

If all our vessels ran'a,
If none but had a crack'a;
If Spanish apes ate all the grapes.
How should we do for sack'a?

If friars had no bald pates,
Nor nuns had no dark cloisters;
If all the seas were beans and peas,
How should we do for oysters?

If there had been no projects,
Nor none that did great wrongs.
If fiddlers still turn players all,
How should we do for songs?

If all things were eternal,
And nothing their end bringing;
If this should be, then how should we,
Here make an end of singing?

ANON 1641

6. *Ye Carpette Knyghte*

I have a horse—a ryghte goode horse—
      Ne doe I envye those
Who scoure ye playne yn headye course
      Tyll soddayne on theyre nose
They lyghte with unexpected force
      Yt ys—a horse of clothes.

I have a saddel—'Say'st thou soe?
                    Wyth styrruppes, Knyghte, to boote?'
I sayde not that—I answere 'Noe'—
                    Yt lacketh such, I woote:
Yt ys a mutton-saddel, loe!
                    Part of ye fleecye brute.

I have a bytte—a ryghte good bytte—
                    As shall bee seene yn tyme.
Ye jawe of horse yt wyll not fytte;
                    Yts use ys more sublyme.
Fayre Syr, how deemest thou of yt?
                    Yt ys—thys bytte of rhyme.

LEWIS CARROLL

7. Spells

I dance and sing without any feet—
This is the spell of the ripening wheat.

With never a tongue I've a tale to tell—
This is the meadow grasses' spell.

I give you health without any fee—
This is the spell of the apple tree.

I rhyme and riddle without any book—
This is the spell of the bubbling brook.

Without any legs I run for ever—
This is the spell of the mighty river.

I fall for ever and not at all—
This is the spell of the waterfall.

Without a voice I roar aloud—
This is the spell of the thunder cloud.

No button or seam has my white coat—
This is the spell of the leaping goat.

I can cheat strangers with never a word—
This is the spell of the cuckoo-bird.

We have tongues in plenty but speak no names—
This is the spell of the fiery flames.

The creaking door has a spell to riddle—
I play a tune without any fiddle.

JAMES REEVES

8. The Song of the Dumb Waiter

Who went to sleep in the flower-bed?
Who let the fire-dog out of the shed?

Who sailed the sauce-boat down the stream?
What did the railway sleeper dream?

Who was it chopped the boot-tree down?
And rode the clothes-horse through the town?

JAMES REEVES

9. A Catch

Seamen three! What men be ye?
Gotham's three wise men we be.
Whither in your bowl so free?
To rake the moon from out the sea.
The bowl goes trim. The moon doth shine.
And our ballast is old wine;
And our ballast is old wine.

Who art thou, so fast adrift?
I am he they call Old Care.
Here on board we will thee lift.
No: I may not enter there.
Wherefore so? 'Tis Jove's decree,
In a bowl Care may not be;
In a bowl Care may not be.

Fear ye not the waves that roll?
No: in a charmed bowl we swim.
What the charm that floats the bowl?
Water may not pass the brim.
The bowl goes trim. The moon doth shine.
And our ballast is old wine;
And our ballast is old wine.

THOMAS LOVE PEACOCK

10. *We are Three*

The Wisemen were but seven, ne'er more shall be for me;
The Muses were but nine, the Worthies three times three;
And three merry boys, and three merry boys, and three
merry boys are we.

The Virtues were but seven, and three the greater be;
The Caesars they were twelve, and the fatal Sisters three;
And three merry girls, three merry girls, three merry girls
are we.

ANON

11. *For a Mocking Voice*

Who calls? Who calls? Who?
Did you call? Did you?—
I call! I call! I!
Follow where I fly.—
Where? O where? O where?
On Earth or in the Air?—
Where you come, I'm gone!
Where you fly, I've flown!—
Stay! ah, stay! ah, stay,
Pretty Elf, and play!
Tell me where you are—
Ha, ha, ha, ha, ha!

ELEANOR FARJEON

226

12. Two Triolets

I ran over a pig
And he seemed quite to like it,
It was in my new gig,
I ran over a pig.
It did not care a fig
Though I saw the wheel strike it.
I ran over a pig
And he seemed quite to like it.

It did not care a fig
I am perfectly certain.
It was such a hard pig
It did not care a fig
For the wheel of the gig
Manufactured at Girton;
It did not care a fig
I am perfectly certain.

Attributed to MAURICE BARING

13. The Common Cormorant

The Common Cormorant or shag
Lays eggs inside a paper bag.
The reason you will see no doubt
It is to keep the lightning out.
But what these unobservant birds
Have never noticed is that herds
Of wandering bears may come with buns
And steal the bags to hold the crumbs.

ANON

14. The Poultries

Let's think of eggs.
They have no legs.
Chickens come from eggs
But they have legs.
The plot thickens;
Eggs come from chickens,
But have no legs under 'em.
What a conundrum!

OGDEN NASH

15. To Be or Not to Be

I sometimes think I'd rather crow
And be a rooster than to roost
And be a crow. But I dunno.

A rooster he can roost also,
Which don't seem fair when crows can't crow.
Which may help some. Still I dunno.

Crows should be glad of one thing, though;
Nobody thinks of eating crow,
While roosters they are good enough
For anyone unless they're tough.

There are lots of tough old roosters though,
And anyway a crow can't crow,
So mebby roosters stand more show.
It looks that way. But I dunno.

ANON

V
TALES,
MARVELLOUS TALES

1. From *The Flower of Old Japan*

Embarkation

When the firelight, red and clear,
    Flutters in the black wet pane,
It is very good to hear
    Howling winds and trotting rain:
It is very good indeed,
    When the nights are dark and cold,
Near the friendly hearth to read
    Tales of ghosts and buried gold.

So with cosy toes and hands
    We were dreaming, just like you;
Till we thought of palmy lands
    Coloured like a cockatoo;
All in drowsy nursery nooks
    Near the clutching fire we sat,
Searching quaint old story-books
    Piled upon the furry mat.

Something haunted us that night
    Like a half-remembered name;
Worn old pages in that light
    Seemed the same, yet not the same;
Curling in the pleasant heat
    Smoothly as a shell-shaped fan,
O! they breathed and smelled so sweet
    When we turned to Old Japan!

Suddenly we thought we heard
    Someone tapping on the wall,
Tapping, tapping like a bird,
    Till a panel seemed to fall
Quietly; and a tall, thin man
    Stepped into the glimmering room,
And he held a little fan,
    And he waved it in the gloom.

Curious reds, and golds, and greens
  Danced before our startled eyes,
Birds from painted Indian screens,
  Beads, and shells, and dragon-flies;
Wings, and flowers, and scent, and flame,
  Fans, and fish, and heliotrope;
Till the magic air became
  Like a dream kaleidoscope.

Then he told us of a land
  Far across a fairy sea;
And he waved his thin white hand
  Like a flower, melodiously;
While a red and blue macaw
  Perched upon his pointed head,
And, as in a dream, we saw
  All the curious things he said.

Tucked in tiny palanquins,
  Magically swinging there,
Flowery-kirtled mandarins
  Floated through the scented air;
Wandering dogs and prowling cats
  Grinned at fish in painted lakes;
Cross-legged conjurors on mats
  Fluted low to listening snakes.

.   .   .   .   .

Ah! but then he waved his fan,
  And he vanished through the wall;
Yet, as in a dream, we ran
  Tumbling after, one and all;
Never pausing once to think,
  Panting after him we sped;
For we saw his robe of pink
  Floating backward as he fled.

Down a secret passage deep,
　　Under roofs of spidery stairs,
Where the bat-winged nightmares creep,
　　And a sheeted phantom glares
Rushed we; ah! how strange it was
　　Where no human watcher stood;
Till we reached a gate of glass
　　Opening on a flowery wood.

Where the rose-pink robe had flown,
　　Borne by swifter feet than ours,
On to Wonder-Wander town,
　　Through the wood of monstrous flowers;
Mailed in monstrous gold and blue
　　Dragon-flies like peacocks fled;
Butterflies like carpets, too,
　　Softly fluttered overhead.

.　　.　　.　　.　　.

Ah, he led us on our road,
　　Showed us Wonder-Wander town;
Then he fled: behind him flowed
　　Once again the rose-pink gown:
Down the long deserted street,
　　All the windows winked like eyes,
And our little trotting feet
　　Echoed to the starry skies.

Low and long for evermore
　　Where the Wonder-Wander sea
Whispers to the wistful shore
　　Purple songs of mystery,
Down the shadowy quay we came—
　　Though it hides behind the hill
You will find it just the same
　　And the seamen singing still.

232

There we chose a ship of pearl,
    And her milky silken sail
Seemed by magic to unfurl
    Puffed before a fairy gale;
Shimmering o'er the purple deep,
    Out across the silvery bar,
Softly as the wings of sleep
    Sailed we towards the morning star.

.　　.　　.　　.　　.

The End of the Quest

Like the dawn upon a dream
    Slowly through the scented gloom
Crept once more the ruddy gleam
    O'er the friendly nursery room.
There, before our waking eyes,
    Large and ghostly, white and dim,
Dreamed the Flower that never dies,
    Opening wide its rosy rim.

Spreading like a ghostly fan,
    Petals white as porcelain,
There the Flower of Old Japan
    Told us we were home again;
For a soft and curious light
    Suddenly was o'er it shed,
And we saw it was a white
    English daisy, ringed with red.

Slowly, as a wavering mist
    Waned the wonder out of sight,
To a sigh of amethyst,
    To a wraith of scented light,
Flower and magic glass had gone;
    Near the clutching fire we sat
Dreaming, dreaming, all alone,
    Each upon a furry mat.

While the firelight, red and clear,
    Fluttered in the black wet pane,
It was very good to hear
    Howling winds and trotting rain.
For we found at last we knew
    More than all our fancy planned,
All the fairy tales were true,
    And home the heart of fairyland.

ALFRED NOYES

2. The Golden Journey to Samarkand

Prologue

We who with songs beguile your pilgrimage
    And swear that Beauty lives though lilies die,
We Poets of the proud old lineage
    Who sing to find your hearts, we know not why,—

What shall we tell you? Tales, marvellous tales
    Of ships and stars and isles where good men rest,
Where nevermore the rose of sunset pales,
    And winds and shadows fall towards the West:

And there the world's first huge white-bearded kings
    In dim glades sleeping, murmur in their sleep,
And closer round their breasts the ivy clings,
    Cutting its pathway slow and red and deep.

II

And how beguile you? Death has no repose
    Warmer and deeper than the Orient sand
Which hides the beauty and bright faith of those
    Who made the Golden Journey to Samarkand.

And now they wait and whiten peaceably,
    Those conquerors, those poets, those so fair:
They know time comes, not only you and I,
    But the whole world shall whiten, here or there;

234

When those long caravans that cross the plain
    With dauntless feet and sound of silver bells
Put forth no more for glory or for gain,
    Take no more solace from the palm-girt wells;

When the great markets by the sea shut fast
    All that calm Sunday that goes on and on:
When even lovers find their peace at last,
    And Earth is but a star, that once had shone.

JAMES ELROY FLECKER

3. From *My Lost Youth*

Often I think of the beautiful town
    That is seated beside the sea;
Often in thought go up and down
The pleasant streets of that dear old town,
    And my youth comes back to me.
        And a verse of a Lapland song
        Is haunting my memory still:
    'A boy's will is the wind's will,
And the thoughts of youth are long, long thoughts.'

I can see the shadowy lines of its trees,
    And catch in sudden gleams,
The sheen of the far-surrounding seas,
The islands that were the Hesperides
    Of all my boyish dreams.
        And the burden of that old song,
        It murmurs and whispers still:
    'A boy's will is the wind's will,
And the thoughts of youth are long, long thoughts.'

I remember the black wharves and the slips,
    And the sea-tides tossing free;
And the Spanish sailors with bearded lips,
And the beauty and mystery of the ships,
    And the magic of the sea.

And the voice of that wayward song
Is singing and saying still:
'A boy's will is the wind's will,
And the thoughts of youth are long, long thoughts.'

I remember the bulwarks by the shore,
And the fort upon the hill;
The sunrise gun, with its hollow roar,
The drum-beat repeated o'er and o'er,
And the bugle wild and shrill.
And the music of that old song
Throbs in my memory still:
'A boy's will is the wind's will,
And the thoughts of youth are long, long thoughts.'

I remember the sea-fight far away,
How it thundered o'er the tide!
And the dead captains, as they lay
In their graves, o'erlooking the tranquil bay,
Where they in battle died.
And the sound of that mournful song
Goes through me with a thrill:
'A boy's will is the wind's will,
And the thoughts of youth are long, long thoughts.'

.   .   .   .

I remember the gleams and glooms that dart
Across the schoolboy's brain;
The song and the silence in the heart,
That in part are prophecies, and in part
Are longings wild and vain.
And the voice of that fitful song
Sings on, and is never still:
'A boy's will is the wind's will,
And the thoughts of youth are long, long thoughts.'

HENRY WADSWORTH LONGFELLOW

236

4. The Mayblossom

(Told me by the pilot)

The ship, *Mayblossom*, left Magellan Straits
And beat into a roaring Northerly.

Slowly she thrust into the strength against her;
The screw raced, the ship trembled, the plates groaned.
Up on her bridge, her Captain and two Mates
Saw in the blindness the Evangelists,
The four great rocks forever standing guard,
All wind-shrieked, sea-swept.

Slowly she beat to westward from the rocks,
Streamed, and turned northward for her Chilean port,
A half-league, then a league, upon her course;
Then, suddenly, the ship's propeller jarred
Off from its shaft and left her helpless there.

She drifted back; the Captain called all hands.
'Men, the propeller's gone; the ship is helpless.
We shall be on the rocks within the hour.
Any of you who choose may take the boats:
I shall stay by her and go down with her.'

Half the ship's people chose to risk the boats.
One boat was smashed to pieces as she lowered.
The other, full of men, got clear away
And with a rag of sail beat from the ship
And no man ever heard of her again.
Meanwhile, the *Mayblossom*
Drifted upon the Four Evangelists;
The wind-shrieked, sea-swept.

Then, as she stumbled in the breakers' backwash,
When the great rocks hung up above the bridge,
And cataracts of billow fell back blind,
And all her fabric trembled from the blows
Of water thwarted by the basalt's face,
A wayward waif of current plucked her clear

237

And swept her South,
Towards the Horn,
To gray seas running forlorn,
Where ships are sown for corn,
And birds have screams in the mouth.

Having a Life and Hope and half a crew,
Captain and Engineer advised together,
Behind the dodger, as she rode the sea.
The Captain said,
'We've forty tons of gunny-sack, in bales,
Down in the forward hold: we might make sails
With that, if we had needles and some twine.
You have no twine or needles, I suppose?'
The Engineer replied, 'We used to use them;
And always, still, when I indent for stores,
I ask to have a hank of twine and needle.
There should be one of each: I'll go to see.'
Soon he came running back with shining eyes.
'Captain, a miracle has happened here:—
I wrote, 'One hank of twine and one sail-needle' . . .
(Things which I never use, one trip in ten),
But by some miracle the chandlers sent
A gross of twine and gross of sail-needles.
See here, assorted sizes, England's best.'
'You cannot beat the good God,' said the Captain,
'For when He gives, He gives beyond all hope.
Now, when we've made some palms we'll buckle-to,
And fashion sails and pluck her out of this.'

They stitched a suit of sails: they contrived yards
From derricks, oars and handspikes: they set sail,
Ran eastward round the Horn and made the Falklands.

There, when the ship-repairers quoted terms,
The Captain told them, 'Rather than pay that,
I'll sail her to the Mainland, and try there.'

So said, so done: he sailed her to the Plate;
Shipped a propeller at a fairer price,
Then, under steam
Trudged the cold blackness of Magellan's stream
To that green water by the Chilean slip
That waited for the shadow of his ship.

JOHN MASEFIELD

5. *Jim*

There was a Boy whose name was Jim;
His Friends were very good to him.
They gave him Tea, and Cakes, and Jam,
And slices of delicious Ham,
And Chocolate with pink inside,
And little Tricycles to ride,
And
        read him Stories through and through,
And even took him to the Zoo—
And there it was the dreadful Fate
Befell him, which I now relate.

You know—at least you *ought* to know,
For I have often told you so—
That Children never are allowed
To leave their Nurses in a Crowd;
Now this was Jim's especial Foible,
He ran away when he was able,
And on this inauspicious day
He slipped his hand and ran away!
He hadn't gone a yard when—
                                        Bang!
With open Jaws a Lion sprang,
And hungrily began to eat
The Boy, beginning at his feet.

Now just imagine how it feels
When first your toes and then your heels,
And then by gradual degrees,
Your shins and ankles, calves and knees,
Are slowly eaten, bit by bit.

No wonder Jim detested it!
No wonder that he shouted 'Hi!'
The Honest Keeper heard his cry,
Though very fat
         he almost ran
To help the little gentleman.
'Ponto!' he ordered, as he came
(For Ponto was the Lion's name),
'Ponto!' he cried,
         with angry Frown.
'Let go, Sir! Down, Sir! Put it down!'
The Lion made a sudden Stop,
He let the Dainty Morsel drop,
And slunk reluctant to his Cage,
Snarling with Disappointed Rage.
But when he bent him over Jim
The Honest Keeper's
         Eyes were dim.
The Lion having reached the head,
The Miserable Boy was dead!

When Nurse informed his Parents, they
Were more Concerned than I can say:—
His Mother, as She dried her eyes,
Said, 'Well—it gives me no surprise,
He would not do as he was told!'
His Father, who was self-controlled,
Bade all the children round attend
To James's miserable end,
And always keep a-hold of Nurse
For fear of finding something worse.

HILAIRE BELLOC

6. *Adventures of Isabel*

Isabel met an enormous bear,
Isabel, Isabel, didn't care;
The bear was hungry, the bear was ravenous,
The bear's big mouth was cruel and cavernous.
The bear said, Isabel, glad to meet you,
How do, Isabel, now I'll eat you!
Isabel, Isabel, didn't worry,
Isabel didn't scream or scurry.
She washed her hands and she straightened her hair up,
Then Isabel quietly ate the bear up.

Once in a night as black as pitch
Isabel met a wicked old witch.
The witch's face was cross and wrinkled,
The witch's gums with teeth were sprinkled.
Ho ho, Isabel! the old witch crowed,
I'll turn you into an ugly toad!
Isabel, Isabel, didn't worry,
Isabel didn't scream or scurry,
She showed no rage and she showed no rancour,
But she turned the witch into milk and drank her.

Isabel met a hideous giant,
Isabel continued self-reliant.
The giant was hairy, the giant was horrid,
He had one eye in the middle of his forehead.
Good morning Isabel, the giant said,
I'll grind your bones to make my bread.
Isabel, Isabel, didn't worry,
Isabel didn't scream or scurry.
She nibbled the zwieback that she always fed off,
And when it was gone, she cut the giant's head off.

Isabel met a troublesome doctor,
He punched and he poked till he really shocked her.
The doctor's talk was of coughs and chills
And the doctor's satchel bulged with pills.

The doctor said unto Isabel,
Swallow this, it will make you well.
Isabel, Isabel, didn't worry,
Isabel didn't scream or scurry.
She took those pills from the pill concocter,
And Isabel calmly cured the doctor.

OGDEN NASH

7. *Incidents in the Life of my Uncle Arly*

O my agèd Uncle Arly!
Sitting on a heap of Barley
        Thro' the silent hours of night,—
Close beside a leafy thicket:—
On his nose there was a Cricket,—
In his hat a Railway-Ticket;—
        (But his shoes were far too tight).

Long ago, in youth, he squander'd
All his goods away, and wander'd
        To the Tiniskoop-hills afar.
There on golden sunsets blazing,
Every evening found him gazing,—
Singing,—'Orb! you're quite amazing!
        How I wonder what you are!'

Like the ancient Medes and Persians,
Always by his own exertions
        He subsisted on those hills;—
Whiles,—by teaching children spelling,—
Or at times by merely yelling,—
Or at intervals by selling
        'Propter's Nicodemus Pills.'

242

Later, in his morning rambles
He perceived the moving brambles—
      Something square and white disclose;—
'Twas a First-class Railway-Ticket;
But, on stooping down to pick it
Off the ground,—a pea-green Cricket
      Settled on my uncle's Nose.

Never—never more,—oh! never,
Did that Cricket leave him ever,—
      Dawn or evening, day or night;—
Clinging as a constant treasure,—
Chirping with a cheerious measure,—
Wholly to my uncle's pleasure,—
      ('Though his shoes were far too tight).

So for three-and-forty winters,
Till his shoes were worn to splinters,
      All those hills he wander'd o'er,—
Sometimes silent;—sometimes yelling;—
Till he came to Borley-Melling,
Near his old ancestral dwelling;—
      (But his shoes were far too tight).

On a little heap of Barley
Died my agèd Uncle Arly,
      And they buried him one night;—
Close beside the leafy thicket:—
There,—his hat and Railway-Ticket;—
There,—his ever-faithful Cricket;—
      (But his shoes were far too tight).

EDWARD LEAR

VI
BATTLES LONG AGO

1. *Lepanto*

White founts falling in the courts of the sun,
And the Soldan of Byzantium is smiling as they run;
There is laughter like the fountains in that face of all men
    feared,
It stirs the forest darkness, the darkness of his beard,
It curls the blood-red crescent, the crescent of his lips,
For the inmost sea of all the earth is shaken with his ships.
They have dared the white republics up the capes of Italy,
They have dashed the Adriatic round the Lion of the Sea,
And the Pope has cast his arms abroad for agony and loss,
And called the kings of Christendom for swords about the
    Cross,
The cold queen of England is looking in the glass;
The shadow of the Valois is yawning at the Mass;
From evening isles fantastical rings faint the Spanish gun,
And the Lord upon the Golden Horn is laughing in the sun.

Dim drums throbbing, in the hills half heard,
Where only on a nameless throne a crownless prince has
    stirred,
Where, risen from a doubtful seat and half-attainted stall,
The last knight of Europe takes weapons from the wall,
The last and lingering troubadour to whom the bird had
    sung,
That once went singing southward when all the world was
    young,
In that enormous silence, tiny and unafraid,
Comes up along a winding road the noise of the Crusade.
Strong gongs groaning as the guns boom far,
Don John of Austria is going to the war,
Stiff flags straining in the night-blasts cold
In the gloom black-purple, in the glint old-gold,
Torchlight crimson on the copper kettle-drums,
Then the tuckets, then the trumpets, then the cannon, and
    he comes.

Don John laughing in the brave beard curled,
Spurning of his stirrups like the thrones of all the world,
Holding his head up for a flag of all the free.
Love-light of Spain—hurrah!
Death-light of Africa!
Don John of Austria
Is riding to the sea.

Mahound is in paradise above the evening star,
(*Don John of Austria is going to the war.*)
He moves a mighty turban on the timeless houri's knees,
His turban that is woven of the sunset and the seas.
He shakes the peacock gardens as he rises from his ease,
And he strides among the tree-tops and is taller than the trees,
And his voice through all the gardens is a thunder sent to bring
Black Azrael and Ariel and Ammon on the wing.
Giants and the Genii,
Multiplex of wing and eye,
Whose strong obedience broke the sky
When Solomon was king.

They rush in red and purple from the red clouds of the morn,
From temples where the yellow gods shut up their eyes in
          scorn;
They rise in green robes roaring from the green hells of the sea
Where fallen skies and evil hues and eyeless creatures be;
On them the sea-valves cluster and the grey sea-forests curl,
Splashed with a splendid sickness, the sickness of the pearl;
They swell in sapphire smoke out of the blue cracks of the
          ground,—
They gather and they wonder and give worship to Mahound.
And he saith, 'Break up the mountains where the hermit-folk
          may hide,
And sift the red and silver sands lest bone of saint abide,
And chase the Giaours flying night and day, not giving rest,
For that which was our trouble comes again out of the west.
We have set the seal of Solomon on all things under sun,
Of knowledge and of sorrow and endurance of things done,

But a noise is in the mountains, in the mountains, and I know
The voice that shook our palaces—four hundred years ago:
It is he that saith not "Kismet"; it is he that knows not Fate;
It is Richard, it is Raymond, it is Godfrey in the gate!
It is he whose loss is laughter when he counts the wager worth,
Put down your feet upon him, that our peace be on the earth.'
For he heard drums groaning and he heard guns jar,
(*Don John of Austria is going to the war.*)
Sudden and still—hurrah!
Bolt from Iberia!
Don John of Austria
Is gone by Alcalar.

St Michael's on his Mountain in the sea-roads of the north
(*Don John of Austria is girt and going forth.*)
Where the grey seas glitter and the sharp tides shift
And the sea folk labour and the red sails lift.
He shakes his lance of iron and he claps his wings of stone;
The noise is gone through Normandy; the noise is gone alone;
The North is full of tangled things and texts and aching eyes
And dead is all the innocence of anger and surprise,
And Christian killeth Christian in a narrow dusty room,
And Christian dreadeth Christ that hath a newer face of doom,
And Christian hateth Mary that God kissed in Galilee,
But Don John of Austria is riding to the sea.
Don John calling through the blast and the eclipse
Crying with the trumpet, with the trumpet of his lips,
Trumpet that sayeth ha!
      Domino gloria!
Don John of Austria
Is shouting to the ships.

King Philip's in his closet with the Fleece about his neck
(*Don John of Austria is armed upon the deck.*)
The walls are hung with velvet that is black and soft as sin,
And little dwarfs creep out of it and little dwarfs creep in.
He holds a crystal phial that has colours like the moon,
He touches, and it tingles, and he trembles very soon,

And his face is as a fungus of a leprous white and grey
Like plants in the high houses that are shuttered from the day,
And death is in the phial, and the end of noble work,
But Don John of Austria has fired upon the Turk.
Don John's hunting, and his hounds have bayed—
Booms away past Italy the rumour of his raid.
Gun upon gun, ha! ha!
Gun upon gun, hurrah!
Don John of Austria
Has loosed the cannonade.

The Pope was in his chapel before day or battle broke,
(*Don John of Austria is hidden in the smoke.*)
The hidden room in a man's house where God sits all the year,
The secret window whence the world looks small and very
    dear.
He sees as in a mirror on the monstrous twilight sea
The crescent of his cruel ships whose name is mystery;
They fling great shadows foe-wards, making Cross and Castle
    dark,
They veil the plumèd lions on the galleys of St Mark;
And above the ships are palaces of brown, black-bearded chiefs,
And below the ships are prisons, where with multitudinous
    griefs,
Christian captives sick and sunless, all a labouring race re-
    pines
Like a race in sunken cities, like a nation in the mines.
They are lost like slaves that swat, and in the skies of morning
    hung
The stairways of the tallest gods when tyranny was young.
They are countless, voiceless, hopeless as those fallen or flee-
    ing on
Before the high Kings' horses in the granite of Babylon.
And many a one grows witless in his quiet room in hell
Where a yellow face looks inward through the lattice of his cell,
And he finds his God forgotten, and he seeks no more a sign—
(*But Don John of Austria has burst the battle-line!*)

Don John pounding from the slaughter-painted poop,
Purpling all the ocean like a bloody pirate's sloop,
Scarlet running over on the silvers and the golds,
Breaking of the hatches up and bursting of the holds,
Thronging of the thousands up that labour under sea
White for bliss and blind for sun and stunned for liberty.
Vivat Hispania!
Domino Gloria!
Don John of Austria
Has set his people free!

Cervantes on his galley sets the sword back in the sheath
(*Don John of Austria rides homeward with a wreath.*)
And he sees across a weary land a straggling road in Spain,
Up which a lean and foolish knight forever rides in vain,
And he smiles, but not as Sultans smile, and settles back the
    blade . . .
(*But Don John of Austria rides home from the Crusade.*)

G. K. CHESTERTON

2. From *The Ballad of Val-ès-Dunes*

(*The victory of William the Conqueror in his youth over the rebels at
Val-ès-Dunes in the year 1047*)

The Horse from Cleres and Valery,
    The Foot from Yvetot,
And all the men of the Harbour Towns
That live by fall and flow.
And all the men of the Beechen Ford
—Oh! William of Falaise, my lord!—
And all the sails in Michael's ward,
And all the shields of Caux,
    Shall follow you out across the world,
    With sword and lance and bow,

To Beachy and to Pevensey Bar,
　　To Chester through the snow,
And sack and pack and camping tent,
　　A-grumbling as they go:
My lord is William of Falaise.
　　Haro!

3. From *Horatius*

And in the nights of winter,
　　When the cold north winds blow,
And the long howling of the wolves
　　Is heard amidst the snow;
When round the lonely cottage
　　Roars loud the tempest's din,
And the good logs of Algidus
　　Roar louder yet within;

When the oldest cask is opened,
　　And the largest lamp is lit;
When the chestnuts glow in the embers
　　And the kid turns on the spit;
When young and old in circle
　　Around the firebrands close;
When the girls are weaving baskets,
　　And the lads are shaping bows;

When the goodman mends his armour,
　　And trims his helmet's plume;
When the goodwife's shuttle merrily
　　Goes flashing through the loom;
With weeping and with laughter
　　Still is the story told,
How well Horatius kept the bridge
　　In the brave days of old.

LORD MACAULAY

250

4. *The Night of Trafalgár*

In the wild October night-time, when the wind raved round
the land,
And the Back-sea met the Front-sea, and our doors were
blocked with sand,
And we heard the drub of Dead-man's Bay, where bones of
thousands are,
We knew not what the day had done for us at Trafalgár.
                    Had done,
                    Had done,
                For us at Trafalgár!

'Pull hard, and make the Nothe, or down we go!' one says,
says he.
We pulled; and bedtime brought the storm; but snug at home
slept we.
Yet all the while our gallants after fighting through the
day,
Were beating up and down the dark, sou'west of Cadiz
Bay.
                    The dark,
                    The dark,
                Sou'west of Cadiz Bay!

The victors and the vanquished then the storm it tossed and
tore,
As hard they strove, those worn-out men, upon that surly
shore;
Dead Nelson and his half-dead crew, his foes from near and
far,
Were rolled together on the deep that night at Trafalgár!
                    The deep,
                    The deep,
                That night at Trafalgár!

THOMAS HARDY

251

5. From *Letters to Malaya iv*

Then came Dunkirk to mitigate the news:
One of those names like Blenheim's, Waterloo's,
Which suddenly Fame in its file writes down;
Unknown one year, the next forever known.
How close to miracle seemed that retreat;
As if, by some blest providential cheat,
Victory had been defeated by defeat,
The winged eluded by the broken-winged!
Yet still our coasts with hazards huge were ringed,
Waiting to strike. For France was prostrate then,
And France's victor marshalling his men
To give his victory its final form.
Eerie the hush in England ere the storm:
Still skies, the stillness heralding disaster;
And one man's voice, the situation's master.
One man whose very blemishes seemed great;
Whose life, had Rome not England been his state,
Plutarch had loved to write, and North translate;
Who time on time in those dumbfounding days
Rallied his country round a famous phrase,
Opposing to the other's frenzied fit
Calm eloquence and chuckle-stirring wit;
For not alone with Nazis was his feud,
Stern foe to Hitler—and to platitude.

. . . For that the poet blesses him indeed—
A minister whose speeches men could read—
But benediction's due for more than that,
The massive head beneath the curious hat,
Exuberant, pugnacious, puckish, bland,
Appeared symbolic of his native land,
As typical of England as its pleasures,
Its poetry, its turf, its weights and measures;
And by such native greatness were we shown
That, isolated, we were not alone:

The glories of our past were our allies;
The Armada had but shifted to the skies;
Churchill was now what Drake and Pitt were then.
Hitler one more of History's wicked men.

MARTYN SKINNER

6. Jack Overdue

Come back, come back, Jolly Jack Straw.
There's ice in the killer sea.
Weather at base closes down for the night:
And the ash-blonde Waaf is waiting tea.

How many long Atlantic hours
He has hunted there alone:
Has he trimly weaved in the silent air
The dullest patrol that's ever flown.

How can they know he found at last
That he made a hunter's strike:
And swooped on a sly swift shark as it dived:
Saw gouting oil mount carpet-like.

Jolly Jack Straw is beating it back,
But his wireless set is blown.
He cannot report his long-sought luck,
Or the ice-dark blinding eye and bone.

Come back, come back, Jolly Jack Straw,
For the ash-blonde Waaf drinks tea;
And the tea leaves tell her fortune as well.
Come back, come back from the killer sea.

JOHN PUDNEY

7. *Watching Post*

A hill flank overlooking the Axe valley.
Among the stubble a farmer and I keep watch
For whatever may come to injure our countryside—
Light-signals, parachutes, bombs, or sea-invaders.
The moon looks over the hill's shoulder, and hope
Mans the old ramparts of an English night.

In a house down there was Marlborough born. One night
Monmouth marched to his ruin out of that valley.
Beneath our castled hill, where Britons kept watch,
Is a church where the Drakes, old lords of this countryside,
Sleep under their painted effigies. No invaders
Can dispute their legacy of toughness and hope.

Two counties away, over Bristol, the searchlights hope
To find what danger is in the air tonight.
Presently gunfire from Portland reaches our valley
Tapping like an ill-hung door in a draught. My watch
Says nearly twelve. All over the countryside
Moon-dazzled men are peering out for invaders.

The farmer and I talk for a while of invaders:
But soon we turn to crops—the annual hope,
Making of cider, prizes for ewes. Tonight
How many hearts along this war-mazed valley
Dream of a day when at peace they may work and watch
The small sufficient wonders of the countryside.

Image or fact, we both in the countryside
Have found our natural law, and until invaders
Come will answer its need: for both of us, hope
Means a harvest from small beginnings, who this night
While the moon sorts out into shadow and shape our valley,
A farmer and a poet, are keeping watch.

C. DAY LEWIS

254

VII
CHRISTMAS CAROLS

1. *On Christmas Day*

(To my Heart)

Today,
Hark! Heaven sings;
  Stretch, tune, my heart!
(For hearts have strings
  May bear their part)
And though thy lute were bruised i' the fall,
Bruised hearts may reach an humble pastoral.

Today,
Shepherds rejoice,
  And angels do
No more: thy voice
  Can reach that too:
Bring then at least thy pipe along,
And mingle consort with the angels' song.

Today
A shed that's thatched
  (Yet straws can sing)
Holds God; God matched
  With beasts; beasts bring
Their song their way: for shame then raise
Thy notes! lambs bleat, and oxen bellow praise.

Today,
God honoured man
  Not angels: yet
They sing; and can
  Raised man forget?
Praise is our debt today, now shall
Angels (man's not so poor) discharge it all?

<pre>
              Today,
       Then, screw thee high,
              My heart, up to
       The angels' cry;
              Sing 'Glory', do:
       What if thy strings all crack and fly?
       On such a ground, music 'twill be to die.
</pre>

CLEMENT PAMAN

2. New Heaven, New War

Come to your heaven, you heavenly choirs!
Earth hath the heaven of your desires;
Remove your dwelling to your God,
A stall is now His best abode;
Sith man their homage doth deny,
Come, angels, all their faults supply.

.   .   .   .   .   .

This little babe so few days old,
Is come to rifle Satan's fold;
And hell doth at His presence quake,
Though He Himself for cold do shake;
For in this weak unarmèd wise
The gates of hell He will surprise.

With tears He fights and wins the field,
His naked breast stands for a shield,
His battering shot are babish cries,
His arrows, looks of weeping eyes,
His martial ensigns, cold and need,
His feeble flesh His warrior's steed.

His camp is pitchèd in a stall,
His bulwark but a broken wall,
The crib His trench, hay-stalks His stakes
Of shepherds He His muster makes;
And thus, as sure His foe to wound,
The angels' trumps alarum sound.

My soul, with Christ join thou in fight;
Stick to the tents that He hath pight;[1]
Within His crib is surest ward,
This little babe will be thy guard;
If thou wilt foil thy foes with joy,
Then flit not from this heavenly boy.

ROBERT SOUTHWELL

3. *Our Lord and Our Lady*

They warned Our Lady for the Child
    That was Our blessed Lord,
And She took Him into the desert wild,
    Over the camel's ford.

And a long song She sang to Him
    And a short story told:
And She wrapped Him in a woollen cloak
    To keep Him from the cold.

But when Our Lord was a grown man
    The Rich they dragged Him down,
And they crucified Him in Golgotha,
    Out and beyond the Town.

They crucified Him on Calvary,
    Upon an April day;
And because He had been Her little Son
    She followed Him all the way.

Our Lady stood beside the Cross,
    A little space apart,
And when She heard Our Lord cry out
    A sword went through Her Heart.

[1] Pitched.

258

They laid Our Lord in a marble tomb,
    Dead, in a winding sheet.
But Our Lady stands above the world
    With the white Moon at Her feet.

HILAIRE BELLOC

4. *Before Dawn*

Dim-berried is the mistletoe
With globes of sheenless grey,
The holly mid ten thousand thorns
Smoulders its fires away;
And in the manger Jesu sleeps
    This Christmas Day.

Bull unto Bull with hollow throat
Makes echo every hill,
Cold sheep in pastures thick with snow
The air with bleatings fill;
While of his mother's heart this Babe
    Takes His sweet will.

All flowers and butterflies lie hid,
The blackbird and the thrush
Pipe but a little as they flit
Restless from bush to bush;
Even to the robin Gabriel hath
    Cried softly, 'Hush!'

Now night is astir with burning stars
In darkness of the snow;
Burdened with frankincense and myrrh
And gold the Strangers go
Into a dusk where one dim lamp
    Burns faintly, Lo!

No snowdrop yet its small head nods,
In winds of winter drear;
No lark at casement in the sky
Sings matins shrill and clear;
Yet in the frozen mirk the Dawn
      Breathes, Spring is here!

WALTER DE LA MARE

5. Christmas Day

Last night in the open shippen
    The Infant Jesus lay,
While cows stood at the hay-crib
    Twitching the sweet hay

As I trudged through the snow-fields
    That lay in their own light,
A thorn-bush with its shadow
    Stood doubled on the night.

And I stayed on my journey
    To listen to the cheep
Of a small bird in the thorn-bush
    I woke from its puffed sleep.

The bright stars were my angels
    And with the heavenly host
I sang praise to the Father,
    The Son and Holy Ghost.

ANDREW YOUNG

6. Children's song of the Nativity

How far is it to Bethlehem?
Not very far.
Shall we find the stable-room
Lit by a star?

Can we see the little child,
Is He within?
If we lift the wooden latch
May we go in?

May we stroke the creatures there,
Ox, ass, or sheep?
May we peep like them and see
Jesus asleep?

If we touch His tiny hand
Will He awake?
Will He know we've come so far
Just for His sake?

Great kings have precious gifts,
And we have naught,
Little smiles and little tears
Are all we brought.

For all weary children
Mary must weep.
Here on His bed of straw
Sleep, children, sleep.

God in His mother's arms,
Babes in the byre,
Sleep, as they sleep who find
Their heart's desire.
                FRANCES CHESTERTON

7. The Old Shepherds

Star of Bethlehem

Do ye remember? . . . Surelye I remember . . .
Were it come April? were it come September?
        Nay friend, nay friend,
        It were the latter end
        Of one December . . .
We cracked our knuckles at the charcoal ember . . .
        Ay, ay 'twas so,
        Amany years ago.

Han't ye fergot the Star? . . . I han't fergotten
Yon Star. Why, wudn't I the first to spot 'un? . . .
     Nay friend, nay friend,
     The merricle-star did wend
     Sky high, an' brought 'un
To some old barton, leaky-roofed an' rotten . . .
     Ay, ay, 'twas so,
     How many years ago?

Why was it? . . . Hey? . . . Why was it? . . . Why, becos it—
Becos it—dang my wamblin' wits! why was it? . . .
     Nay friend, nay friend,
     Leave cudgellin', go tend
     Thy yowes, an' closet
The yeanlings in new straw . . . Bless us, why was it
     Yon Star came so
     A mort o' years ago? . . .

ELEANOR FARJEON

VIII
EVENING AND
THE THREAT OF BED

1. Saturday Afternoon

They have gone home now, the labourers;
The field in stook
Lies open to the sky, which draws near mistily
And blurs that ageless book.

Now golden Time is lengthening to Eternity;
Young hands have gone to town.
There is nobody in the cornfields on a Saturday
To watch the sun sink tired behind the down.

Beautiful is the ebb tide, the evening,
When Earth forgives
Her sons of blood and iron their skin-deep mastery,
And breathes, and lives.

LILIAN BOWES LYON

2. Sowing

It was a perfect day
For sowing; just
As sweet and dry was the ground
As tobacco-dust.

I tasted deep the hour
Between the far
Owl's chuckling first soft cry
And the first star.

A long stretched hour it was;
Nothing undone
Remained; the early seeds
All safely sown

264

And now, hark at the rain,
Windless and light,
Half a kiss, half a tear,
Saying good-night.

EDWARD THOMAS

3. *Night of Spring*

Slow, horses, slow,
As through the wood we go—
    We would count the stars in heaven,
Hear the grasses grow:

Watch the cloudlets few
Dappling the deep blue,
    In our open palms outspread
Catch the blessëd dew.

Slow, horses, slow,
As through the wood we go—
    We would see fair Dian ride
With her huntress bow:

We would hear the breeze
Ruffling the dim trees,
    Hear its sweet love-ditty set
To endless harmonies.

Slow, horses, slow,
As through the wood we go—
    All the beauty of the night
We would learn and know!

THOMAS WESTWOOD

4. An Evening Walk

I never saw a lovelier sky;
The faces of the passers-by
Shine with gold light as they step west
As though by secret joy possessed,
Some rapture that is not of earth
But in that heavenly climate has its birth.

I know it is the sunlight paints
The faces of these travelling saints,
But shall I hold in cold misprision
The calm and beauty of that vision
Upturned a moment from the sorrow
That makes today today, tomorrow tomorrow.

ANDREW YOUNG

5. Don Juan's Address to the Sunset

Exquisite stillness! What serenities
Of earth and air! How bright atop the wall
The stone-crop's fire, and beyond the precipice
How huge, how hushed, the primrose evenfall!
How softly, too, the white crane voyages
Yon honeyed height of warmth and silence, whence
He can look down on islet, lake and shore
And voiceless woods and pathless promontories,
Or, further gazing, view the magnificence
Of cloudlike mountains and of mountainous cloud
Or ghostly wrack below the horizon rim
Not even his eye has vantage to explore.
Now, spirit, find out wings and mount to him,
Wheel where he wheels, where he is soaring soar,
Hang where now he hangs in the planisphere—
Evening's first star and golden as a bee
In the sun's hair—for happiness is here!

ROBERT NICHOLS

266

6. Fireflies in the garden

Here come real stars to fill the upper skies,
And here on earth come emulating flies,
That though they never equal stars in size,
(And they were never really stars at heart)
Achieve at times a very star-like start.
Only, of course, they can't sustain the part.

ROBERT FROST

7. From *Songs of the Night Watches*

'Come out and hear the waters shoot, the owlet hoot, the
   owlet hoot;
  Yon crescent moon, a golden boat, hangs dim behind the
   tree, O!
The dropping thorn makes white the grass, O sweetest lass,
   and sweetest lass;
  Come out and smell the ricks of hay adown the croft with
   me, O!'

JEAN INGELOW

8. No Bed

No bed! no bed! we shouted,
And wheeled our eyes from home
To where the green and golden woods
    Cried, Come!

Wild sang the evening birds,
The sun-clouds shone in our eyes,
A silver snippet of moon hung low
    In the skies.

We ran, we leapt, we sang,
We yodelled loud and shrill,
Chased Nobody through the valley and
    Up the hill.

267

We laughed, we quarrelled, we drank
The cool sweet of the dew,
Beading on bud and leaf the dim
    Woods through.

We stayed, we listened, we looked—
Now dark was on the prowl!
Too-whit-a-woo, from its hollow called
    An owl . . .

O Sleep, at last to slide
Into eyes made drunk with light;
Call in thy footsore boys to harmless
    Night!

          WALTER DE LA MARE

9. *Escape at Bedtime*

The lights from the parlour and kitchen shone out
    Through the blinds and the windows and bars;
And high overhead all moving about,
    There were thousands and millions of stars.
There ne'er were such thousands of leaves on a tree,
    Nor of people in church or the Park,
As the crowd of the stars that looked down upon me,
    And that glittered and winked in the dark.

The Dog, and the Plough, and the Hunter, and all,
    And the star of the sailor, and Mars,
These shone in the sky, and the pail by the wall
    Would be half full of water and stars.
They saw me at last, and they chased me with cries,
    And they soon had me packed into bed;
But the glory kept shining and bright in my eyes,
    And the stars going round in my head.

          ROBERT LOUIS STEVENSON

IX
THE DAY ENDS

1. *Birthright*

Lord Rameses of Egypt sighed
    Because a summer evening passed;
And little Ariadne cried
    That summer fancy fell at last
To dust; and young Verona died
    When beauty's hour was overcast.

Theirs was the bitterness we know
    Because the clouds of hawthorn keep
So short a state, and kisses go
    To tombs unfathomably deep,
While Rameses and Romeo
    And little Ariadne sleep.

JOHN DRINKWATER

2. From *Twilight Calm*

Oh pleasant eventide!
    Clouds on the western side
Grow grey and greyer, hiding the warm sun:
The bees and birds, their happy labours done,
    Seek their close nests and bide.

Screened in the leafy wood
    The stock-doves sit and brood:
The very squirrel leaps from bough to bough
But lazily; pauses; and settles now
    Where once he stored his food.

One by one the flowers close,
    Lily and dewy rose
Shutting their tender petals from the moon:
The grasshoppers are still; but not so soon
    Are still the noisy crows.

The dormouse squats and eats
Choice little dainty bits
Beneath the spreading roots of a broad lime;
Nibbling his fill he stops from time to time
And listens where he sits.

From far the lowings come
Of cattle driven home:
From farther still the wind brings fitfully
The vast continual murmur of the sea,
Now loud, now almost dumb.

The gnats whirl in the air,
The evening gnats; and there
The owl opes broad his eyes and wings to sail
For prey; the bat wakes; and the shell-less snail
Comes forth, clammy and bare.

Hark! that's the nightingale,
Telling the self-same tale
Her song told when the ancient earth was young:
So echoes answered when her song was sung
In the first wooded vale.

We call it love and pain,
The passion of her strain;
And yet we little understand or know:
Why should it rather not be joy that so
Throbs in each throbbing vein?

CHRISTINA ROSSETTI

3. *Alone*

Twilight over the sea and no ship in sight,
The sky blown clear of cloud, and the coming night
Gathering shade by shade; all the winds that blow
Sending the waves one way, tossing their tops to snow,

To foam that falls and slides over the curling crest,
Spreading in marble-pattern under the dark blue breast
Of the wave. No star, no bird, only the wind blowing
Strong from the darkening sky and all the waves going,
Running away to the north, freshly crowned with white
Glimmering in the lonely time between the dusk and the
    night.

STELLA GIBBONS

4. From *Night*

The sun descending in the west,
The evening star does shine;
The birds are silent in their nest,
And I must seek for mine.
The moon, like a flower,
In heaven's high bower,
With silent delight
Sits and smiles on the night.

WILLIAM BLAKE

5. *Evening in February*

The windy evening drops a grey
Old eyelid down across the sun,
The last crow leaves the ploughman's way,
And happy lambs make no more fun.

Wild parsley buds beside my feet,
A doubtful thrush makes hurried tune,
The steeple in the village street
Doth seem to pierce the twilight moon.

I hear and see those changing charms,
For all—my thoughts are fixed upon
The hurry and the loud alarms
Before the fall of Babylon.

FRANCIS LEDWIDGE

6. *Night*

That shining moon—watched by that one faint star:
Sure now am I, beyond the fear of change,
The lovely in life is the familiar,
And only the lovelier for continuing strange.

WALTER DE LA MARE

7. *For Sleep or Death*

Cure me with quietness,
Bless me with peace;
Comfort my heaviness,
Stay me with ease.
Stillness in solitude
Send down like dew;
Mine armour of fortitude
Piece and make new:
That when I rise again
I may shine bright
As the sky after rain,
Day after night.

RUTH PITTER

8. From *Life*

Life! I know not what thou art,
But know that thou and I must part;
And when, or how, or where we met,
I own to me's a secret yet.

• • • • • •

Life! we've been long together,
Through pleasant and through cloudy weather;
'Tis hard to part when friends are dear;
Perhaps 'twill cost a sigh, a tear;
Then steal away, give little warning,
Choose thine own time;
Say not Good night, but in some brighter clime
Bid me Good morning.

ANNA LETITIA BARBAULD

Index of Authors and Biographical Notes

Born in 1907 at York. Educated at Gresham's School, Holt, and Christ Church, Oxford. During the nineteen-thirties he was the leader of a group of 'Left-wing' poets that included C. Day Lewis and Stephen Spender. With Christopher Isherwood he collaborated in writing poetic dramas. He served during the war in Spain as a stretcher-bearer on the Republican side. He has been a schoolmaster in England and Scotland. In 1938 he went to the United States; became a naturalized American, and Professor of English Literature at the Ann Arbor University, Michigan. It was while working for documentary films in this country that he wrote *Night Mail* as part of the script for a film made by the G.P.O. Film Unit.

Born and educated in England, but when she was fifteen she went out to Malacca. She has spent the greater part of her life in Malaya as both her father and husband were Malayan Civil Servants. For her three sons she has written several books of poems (*The Joyful Way* and *Dance and Sing*) and stories, *The Talking House*, *The Three Rings*, and *The Herewegoes*. The last two of these are about the jungle through which she has made many expeditions. She now lives in Kent and has five grandchildren.

Born in 1743 at Kibworth Harcourt, Leicestershire. Educated at home. Her brother collected her poems and arranged their publication in 1773. She married a clergyman schoolmaster and taught in his school at Palgrave in Suffolk. Later in life they moved to Hampstead where she tutored private pupils. She wrote numerous books for children, lessons, essays, and improving tales as well as her poetry. She died in 1825.

Born in 1874, the eighth son of Lord Revelstoke. He had a French governess who encouraged his early love of France. He went to

Eton and Oxford (where he met Hilaire Belloc). In *The Puppet Show of Memory* he tells the story of his happy childhood. He went into the Diplomatic Service, and was with the Royal Flying Corps during the First World War. The lines here, from *Diffugere Nives*, are part of an elegy on the death of his nephew, Cecil Spenser, who was killed by a fall from his pony. Lawrence of Arabia wrote when he had read the poem: 'You have a gift, the great gift, of just putting out your finger, effortlessly, to touch us in the heart.'

Thomas Lovell Beddoes   19

Born in 1803, the son of a distinguished physician who died when Thomas was five. His aunt was Maria Edgeworth who wrote many books for boys and girls. Educated at Charterhouse and at Oxford, he then studied medicine. He specialized in macabre poetry and his best-known book is called *Death's Jestbook*. In 1849 he committed suicide.

Hilaire Belloc   2, 34, 58, 76, 187, 239, 249, 258

Born in France in 1870, but educated in England. He achieved a First in Honour History Schools at Balliol College, Oxford. From 1906 to 1910 he was Member of Parliament for Salford South. In 1896 *The Bad Child's Book of Beasts* was first published. He wrote numerous works; history, biography, essays, novels, poetry, criticism, a book about sailing his own boat, *The Cruise of the Nona*, and a book about a journey to Rome on foot, *The Path to Rome*. A. G. Macdonell described Belloc as 'the greatest master of English prose and poetry in our time'. He died in 1953.

John Betjeman   75, 95

Born in 1906 and educated at Marlborough and Oxford. He has made a name as poet, critic, and broadcaster, mainly on architectural subjects. He is the editor and author of guide books; reviews novels for the *Daily Telegraph*; and was literary editor for *Time and Tide*. He is married and has one son and one daughter. His gift is for finding matter for poetry in the most unpromising surroundings. 'I love suburbs and gas light and Pont Street and Gothic Revival Churches and mineral railways, provincial towns and garden cities.' Trebetherick, about which he writes here, is on the other side of the estuary from Padstow in Cornwall. Horsey Mere is in Norfolk: part of the Norfolk Broads, separated by a narrow strip of sandy land from the open North Sea.

Laurence Binyon

Born in Lancaster in 1869. Educated at St Paul's School and Trinity College, Oxford. He worked in the British Museum and became Professor of Poetry at Harvard. He was an authority on Oriental Art, and a writer of books on fine art, as well as plays, poems and critical studies of literature. In 1890 he won the Newdigate prize. As a schoolboy he wrote poems that were praised by Robert Browning and Matthew Arnold. He died in 1943.

William Blake

Born 1757. He was the son of a London hosier, did not go to school, but was apprenticed to an engraver to the Society of Antiquaries. This gave him the training which led him to illustrate much of his work with his own engravings. Many of these are symbolic or mystical, both in verse and prose. He is perhaps best known for his *Songs of Innocence* and *Songs of Experience* (from which comes 'Tiger; Tiger; burning bright'), and for his Song, 'Jerusalem'. He illustrated with engravings works other than his own and he is as celebrated for his poetry as for his art. He died in 1827.

Gordon Bottomley

Born in 1874 at Keighley in Yorkshire. He was educated at the Grammar School there, lived most of his life on the edge of the Lake District and married a neighbour's daughter. His first verses were published in 1896. In 1923 he won the *Femina Vie Heureuse* prize and in 1925 the Benson Medal for poetry. The main work of his life was the revival of English verse drama. He suffered from ill health all his life, and died in 1948.

Robert Bridges

Born in Walmer, Kent, in 1844, educated at Eton and Oxford. He qualified and practised as a doctor but in 1882 gave up medicine for literature. In 1913 he was made Poet Laureate. He was a friend of Gerard Manley Hopkins, and introduced his poems to the public in 1918 after the poet's death. He published numerous volumes of poetry and criticism; perhaps his most important work was his last, *The Testament of Beauty*, a long philosophical poem which appeared when he was eighty-five. He died in 1930.

Emily Brontë 192

Born at Hartshead, Yorkshire, in 1818. She lived at Haworth
Parsonage (except for a short time when she worked as a governess)
all her life. She was sister of Charlotte, Anne, and Branwell. She
wrote a great deal of poetry, some of which was published in her
lifetime in a small volume together with verses by Charlotte and
Anne. She wrote one remarkable novel, *Wuthering Heights*. She died
in 1848 of tuberculosis.

Rupert Brooke 167

Born in 1887 at Rugby. His father was a housemaster at Rugby
School. He was educated there and at King's College, Cambridge.
In 1910 he was living at Grantchester, writing, reading, and visiting
London where he met, through the friendship of Sir Edward Marsh,
many young poets of the day. He travelled in Europe and round the
world, spending several months in the South Seas. When the First
World War broke out he joined the Army and died during the
campaign at the Dardanelles. His first poems were published in
1905, and his collected poems, with a memoir by Edward Marsh,
in 1918.

Elizabeth Barrett Browning 3

Born at Coxhoe Hall, Durham, in 1806. The family later moved
to Wimpole Street. She was always delicate and her eccentric father
confined her to the house, treating her as a permanent invalid. She
was an established poet in her own right at the time of her meeting
with Robert Browning in 1846. They eloped together and after
their marriage lived in Italy where she died in 1861. She was given
a golden cocker spaniel puppy, Flush, by Miss Mitford, and Virginia
Woolf has written a life of Elizabeth as it might have been seen
through the eyes of her dog.

Robert Browning 48

Born in Camberwell in 1812, the son of a clerk at the Bank of
England. He had private tutors till he went to University College,
London. His first work, *Pauline*, was published when he was twenty-
one and his last, *Asolando*, appeared on the day of his death. He was
brought up 'in a library', and was one of the best read of English
poets. He so enjoyed the sound of words that he sometimes forgot

their sense. In 1846 he married Elizabeth Barrett after a romantic love affair. He rescued her from Wimpole Street and took her to Italy. He died in 1889 in Venice and is buried in Westminster Abbey.

Gerald Bullett 97, 100

Born in 1893. Published his first novel in 1914 and his most recent one in 1952. He served during the First World War and afterwards became novelist, critic, essayist, and poet. He has contributed to many journals, and has written three books for children. He is married, lives in Sussex, and has one daughter. His poems are contained in two volumes, *Poems* and *News From the Village*. He contributes to Children's Hour and is a frequent broadcaster of his own short stories and overseas book talks.

George Gordon, Lord Byron 215

Born in Harrow in 1788. He was born lame and was a crippled, fattish, timid boy who became a passionate young man. Poetry was his safety valve. Hazlitt wrote of him, '. . . whether he is in his bath, in his study, or on horseback, he writes as habitually as others talk or think, and we always find the spirit of the man of genius breathing from his verse'. Byron died of fever in Greece while fighting with the Greeks for their independence in 1824.

Roy Campbell 161

Born in 1901 in Durban. Educated at Durban High School and Natal University. He is a man of action as well as a poet. He fought in Spain on the side of General Franco, and during the Second World War was in East and North Africa. He has lived most of his adult life in France, Spain (he is an accomplished bullfighter), and Portugal, mostly doing something 'in the horse line'. His autobiography, *Light on a Dark Horse*, was published recently. He now lives in London. In 1952 he was awarded the Foyle Prize for Poetry.

Edward Capern 118, 125

Born at the beginning of the nineteenth century, he was a country postman who wrote poetry in his spare time. He was employed all his life on the letter round from Bideford to Buckland Brewer in Devon, at a salary of 10*s*. 6*d*. a week. An eminent stationer of Walbrook became interested in his poems, and secured for him the patronage of the wealthy. His poems were collected and published in 1856. He visited and was visited by many literary celebrities of the day; he knew Charles Kingsley and Froude the historian, was given books by Landor, and had a copy of her *Poems* from Eliza Cook. He was a 'sound, hale and hearty Englishman' who invariably wore a black bowler jauntily on the side of his head.

Lewis Carroll 56, 221, 223

Born in 1832, son of the Rector of Daresbury in Cheshire. His real name was Charles Lutwidge Dodgson. As a boy he invented many games for his brothers and sisters and owned a marionette theatre. He went to school at Rugby, where he contributed to manuscript magazines pieces that in a slightly altered form appeared in *Alice*. He became lecturer in Mathematics at Christ Church, Oxford. His first books to be published were treatises on mathematics. Then came some humorous verse. Although he lived alone in college, he was fond of children and his hobby was taking their photographs. One of his favourites was Alice Liddell, the original of the Wonderland Alice. *The Mad Gardener's Song* comes from *Sylvie and Bruno*, the book that he was writing when he died in 1898.

Frances Chesterton 260

The wife of G. K. Chesterton. She was a Miss Frances Blogg. Of his first impression of her Chesterton wrote, 'a Juno-like creature in a tremendous hat who eyed him all the time half-wildly, like a shying horse, because he said he was quite happy'. They were married in Kensington Parish Church in June 1901 and lived at first in a flat in Battersea and later at Beaconsfield in Bucks. Mrs Chesterton died in 1938.

Gilbert Keith Chesterton 14, 20, 214, 245

Born in London in 1874. He went to St Paul's School and afterwards studied art at the Slade. He gave this up to work in a publisher's office and from there left to become a Fleet Street journalist. In 1901 he married and moved from Battersea to Beaconsfield. From 1905 till 1930 he wrote an essay a week for the *Illustrated London News*, missing only two in twenty-five years. He wrote novels, essays, plays, biographies, histories, detective stories (he invented

Father Brown), as well as poetry. Belloc considered *Lepanto* 'the summit of high rhetorical verse in all our generation'. Chesterton died at Beaconsfield in 1936.

Richard Church   84, 154, 181, 188

Born in 1893, the son and grandson of Civil Servants. Educated at Dulwich Hamlet School. Worked in the Civil Service for twenty-four years, then became active in the literary world as poet, novelist, and critic. He has now published nine novels and fourteen books of verse. He lives in an oast-house in Kent, works as literary adviser to a publisher and is Director of the English Festival of Spoken Poetry. He has written several books for children including *The Cave* and *Dog Toby*.

John Clare   171

Born in 1793, the son of a crippled farm labourer. He worked on the land, became a militiaman, and then a tramp. In 1820 a book-seller in Stamford helped him to get his first book of poems published. As a result of this he was helped by a nobleman, who liked his work, financed him, and gave him a farm. He failed to make a success of this, and eventually went mad. It was when he was in the asylum at Northampton that some of his best poetry was written. He died in 1864.

Arthur Hugh Clough   155

Born in 1819, the son of a Liverpool cotton merchant. He was educated at Rugby and Oriel College, Oxford. He became a Fellow of Oriel and later Principal of University Hall, London, and an Examiner in the Education Office. He died in Florence in 1861.

Mary Coleridge   21, 114, 174

A great-niece of Samuel Taylor Coleridge. Born in 1861. She published poems during her lifetime but only under a pseudonym. Her work was collected by Henry Newbolt and published under her own name in 1907. Robert Bridges wrote of her poems that they 'often exhibit imagination of a very rare kind. It is their intimacy and spontaneity that gives them so great value.' She died in 1907.

Samuel Taylor Coleridge

Born in Ottery St Mary, Devon, in 1772. His father was Vicar. He went to school at Christ's Hospital and finished his education at Cambridge, in a dragoon regiment (he fell off his horse frequently and particularly disliked grooming it), and at the University of Göttingen in north Germany. He settled near Wordsworth in the Lake District and contributed his long poem *The Ancient Mariner* to the *Lyrical Ballads*. In 1810 he left the Lakes for London where he lived till his death in 1834. He was unhappy in his marriage and towards the end of his life took to opium. He had three sons with unlikely names, Hartley, Berkeley, and Derwent.

Abraham Cowley

Born in 1618 in Fleet Street, the son of a stationer. He began writing poetry at the age of ten. He published two slim volumes of poems while he was still at school at Winchester. Later he went to Trinity College, Cambridge, but was ejected by the Parliamentarians as a Royalist in 1643. He went as secretary to the Queen when she fled to France and deciphered the letters between her and Charles I. He was sent for a time to England as a Royalist spy. He was greatly interested in science, and was one of the first Members of the Royal Society. After the Restoration, he retired to an estate at Chertsey where his chief occupations were botany and poetry. He never married. In 1667 he died and is buried in Westminster Abbey.

William Cowper

Born in 1731 in Berkhamsted, Herts, where his father was Rector. He was educated at Winchester and studied Law. He was called to the Bar in 1754, but never practised. He was a shy, erratic person who was liable to periods of insanity. He lived first at Olney in Bucks and broke his heart over two unsuccessful love affairs. He made various attempts at suicide. He did not start writing poetry until he was fifty, when he found solace in a quiet country existence, gardening, carpentering, writing poetry, and looking after his beloved hares. He was one of the great letter writers. Perhaps his best-known work is *John Gilpin*, but mainly his poetry is about simple domestic things. He died in 1800.

W. H. Davies 205, 208

Born in 1870 in a public house in Newport, Monmouthshire. His father died when he was a child and his mother married again leaving him to the care of his grandparents. 'Our home consisted of grandfather, grandmother, an imbecile brother, a sister, myself, a maidservant, a dog, a cat, a parrot, a dove and a canary bird.' He often played truant from school but before he left became captain of the rugger team. At fourteen he was apprenticed to a picture-frame maker, but after his apprenticeship went off to sea, reached America, and lived the life of a tramp. When he lost a leg in an accident while hitch-hiking on a train, he returned to England, lived in poverty in London, and at the age of thirty-four began writing poetry. He had his verses printed and peddled them from door to door. Gradually he gained recognition and was awarded a Civil List Pension. He married, and in 1917 settled in the country. He has written his own life story in *The Autobiography of a Super-Tramp*. He died in 1940.

Geoffrey Dearmer 5, 168

Is the son of the Rev Dr Percy Dearmer. He was born in London and educated at Westminster School and Christ Church, Oxford. He is an Examiner of plays to the Lord Chamberlain and is the Editor of the 'Children's Hour' Department of the B.B.C. in London. He has published novels and plays, and much verse and literary journalism.

Paul Dehn 103

Born on Guy Fawkes Day 1912. Educated at Shrewsbury and Brasenose College, Oxford. He has published two books of poems, *The Day's Alarm* and *Romantic Landscape*. He is a film critic and frequently broadcasts. His hobby is watching birds.

Walter de la Mare 8, 15, 27, 116, 127, 136, 206, 259, 267, 273

Born in Kent in 1873. Went to St Paul's Choir School and afterwards worked for the Anglo-Iranian Oil Company for eighteen years in the city. His first book, *Songs of Childhood*, was published under the pseudonym Walter Ramal in 1902. He wrote stories, novels, criticism and essays as well as poetry. He compiled four remarkable anthologies; one, of poems and verses for children of all ages, *Come Hither*, has as introduction perhaps the best story he has ever written. His verses for children have been published in two volumes *Peacock Pie* and *Bells and Grass*. Received the Order of Merit in the Coronation and Birthday Honours, 1953. He died in 1956.

Thomas Deloney   41

Born about 1543, a silk-weaver by trade. He lived in Norwich where he wrote and published, mainly in papers, ballads on the happenings of the day. These won him wide popularity at the time. Two collections of them were published after his death. He also wrote fiction. He died in 1600 or thereabouts.

Emily Dickinson   163, 206

Born in 1830 in Amherst, U.S.A., one of a group of towns that spread west and south of Boston. Her father was a sinister man who disapproved of her writing poetry, frowned at her jokes and forbade her to marry. She became a recluse, so shy that she could not bear to meet her closest friends. She wrote letters to them, and these have been collected and published. In one she writes, 'I find ecstasy in living, the mere sense of living is joy enough. To live is startling, it leaves but little room for other occupations'. She died in 1886.

John Drinkwater   144, 166, 270

Born in 1882. Educated at Oxford High School and Birmingham University. 'I cannot remember that I took any particular interest in anything in the classrooms, or that anyone took any particular interest in me. But I acquired an enthusiasm for games that I have never lost. I was, I think, the youngest boy to get colours in both the cricket and football elevens of my time and I am quite unreasonably proud of the fact that I made a record for the junior long jump that has stood for fifteen years.' His hobby was collecting stamps. For twelve years he was an insurance clerk, then began writing plays. He wrote several, mainly on historical subjects. The first to be performed was *Abraham Lincoln* in 1918. He then published many volumes of verse, including two for children, biographies and critical studies. He died in 1937.

Born in 1888 in St Louis, Missouri. Educated at Harvard, the Sorbonne, and Merton College, Oxford. In 1913 he came to London and in 1927 became a naturalized Englishman. He worked in a bank and was a schoolmaster at Highgate, and is a director of the publishing firm of Faber & Faber. His first volumes of poetry, *Prufrock* in 1917 and *The Waste Land* in 1922, were ahead of most of his critics but have deeply influenced contemporary poetry. He is the author of plays and books of literary criticism, and one book of humorous verses, *Old Possum's Book of Practical Cats.*

Eleanor Farjeon   26, 37, 81, 99, 129, 149, 225, 261

Born in 1881 in London. She never went to school but her parents knew everyone in the Bohemian literary and dramatic world so she grew up in an atmosphere rich with imaginative suggestion. She began writing her own works on a typewriter at the age of seven. When she was sixteen she wrote the libretto of an opera called *Fioretta* which had music by her brother and was produced at the Royal Academy of Music. Her first successes in poetry were two books of *Nursery Rhymes of London Town.* She has since written plays, novels, music, children's tales and games and the sort of books that fit into no category but are enjoyed by all generations, like *Martin Pippin in the Apple Orchard* and *The New Book of Days.* She lives in a cottage in the old part of Hampstead. Her latest volume of collected verses is called *Silver-sand and Snow.*

James Elroy Flecker   234

Born in Lewisham in 1884. Educated at Uppingham and Trinity College, Oxford. He studied oriental languages, entered the consular service and was sent to Constantinople in 1910. He was vice-consul in Beirut in 1911. In 1915 he died of consumption in Switzerland. *The Golden Journey to Samarkand* was written 'with the single intention of creating beauty.'

Robert Frost   15, 33, 101, 108, 172, 186, 267

Born in California in 1875. His father died when he was ten. When he was fourteen he started reading and writing poetry. His first job was as a mill hand and later he supplemented his income by teaching and farming. In 1912 he came to England with his wife and four children and when his first book of poems, *A Boy's Will*, was published he began to meet contemporary poets and writers. Till 1915 he farmed near Ledbury in Gloucestershire, returning then to America where he now lives. His *Collected Poems* were published in 1930 and *A Further Range* in 1936.

Viola Gerard Garvin 207

Born in Newcastle-upon-Tyne in 1898. She grew up in London, one of a big family of brothers and sisters, in a home crammed with books. In 1916 she left school and went to Somerville College to read English, and this she afterwards taught. In 1926 she became Literary Editor of the *Observer*, of which her famous father J. L. Garvin was then Editor. Her first book of verse, *Dedications*, was published in 1928. During the 1939 war she worked for the exiled Polish government. Now she reviews novels for the *Daily Telegraph*, reads 'books about Nature, about drawing and painting, about history, about Chile, and always poetry', and is collecting for publication another volume of her own poems.

David Gascoyne 111

Born in 1916 in Harrow, Middlesex. He went to school in the Close at Salisbury, and for six years was a chorister in the Cathedral choir. His first poems were printed in the school magazine. He wrote a novel *Opening Day* which was published before his seventeenth birthday. For six years before the war he lived in Paris and wrote a book about the poets and painters of the Surrealist movement. During the war he was a ship's cook and acted for ENSA.

Stella Gibbons 21, 165, 216, 271

Born in 1902 in a poor district of London where her father was a doctor. She and her two brothers used to escape whenever they could (they did not go to school) into the yard of the pencil-making factory at the back of their house, and play at spies in the stacks of planks and boards used for making pencils. She is married and has one daughter. Of her many novels perhaps the best known is *Cold Comfort Farm*. She has published, as well as her poetry, a story for children, *The Untidy Gnome*.

Oliver St John Gogarty   81, 142, 211

Born in 1878. Educated at Stonyhurst and Trinity College, Dublin. He was a Senator of the Irish Free State from 1922 to 1936. He has been doctor, athlete, and airman, as well as poet and novelist. He was a friend of 'Æ' (the Irish poet G. W. Russell) and W. B. Yeats. During the Civil War in Ireland he was captured by the Republicans and imprisoned in a house by the Liffey. He escaped by swimming the river and in the midst of the flood promised it two swans if he survived. Later he telephoned W. B. Yeats to ask where he could buy two swans. A collected edition of his poems was published in 1952.

Edmund Gosse   71

Born in London in 1849. His parents were Plymouth Brethren. His mother died when he was seven and his home was a gloomy place. In his novel *Father and Son*, he has written about his childhood. In 1867, through the influence of Charles Kingsley, he was appointed as assistant librarian to the British Museum. In 1875 he moved to the Board of Trade where he was employed as a translator. He became the friend of nearly every leading writer of his time. He wrote plays, verse, a novel, and essays, but was best known as a literary critic. He lectured for a time in English Literature at Trinity College, Cambridge. He married in 1875 and had a son and two daughters. He was knighted in 1925 and died in 1928.

Virginia Graham   99

Daughter of Harry Graham who wrote *Ruthless Rhymes for Heartless Homes*. She is married to Antony Thesiger, lives in London, and has no children or pets. She writes film reviews for *The Spectator* and poems for *Punch*. She has published two books of humorous essays. She does not enjoy writing and prefers going to the theatre, reading, playing tennis or tatting. This poem originally appeared in *Collins Magazine*.

Robert Graves   16

Born in 1895 and brought up in a home that was full of children and books. His father married twice, he was the third of five children by the second wife, and there were five by the first. Educated at Charterhouse and St John's College, Oxford. During the First

World War he served in the Royal Welch Fusiliers with Siegfried Sassoon. He wrote about his experiences in the war in *Goodbye to All That*. In 1934 he won the James Tait Black and Hawthornden Prizes with *I, Claudius*. Between the wars he worked in Majorca, and has now returned there.

Julian Grenfell 177

Born in 1888, son of Lord Desborough. Educated at Eton and Balliol. He joined the Army and was commissioned in 1910. He was killed in France during the First World War. His fame rests mainly on one magnificent poem, *Into Battle*.

Thomas Hardy 112, 119, 251

Born in 1840 near Dorchester, the son of a builder. He began a career as an architect but turned to literature in 1871, when *Desperate Remedies*, his first novel, was published. His novels met with increasing success until the appearance of *Jude the Obscure*. Criticism of this book drove Hardy to poetry. His first volume, *Wessex Poems*, was published in 1898, then came the epic drama *The Dynasts*, in three parts. *Winter Words*, a final collection of poems, appeared after his death in 1928. He married twice, and lived all his life within reach of Dorchester.

W. E. Henley 60

Born in Gloucestershire in 1849. He was crippled from childhood. He edited several periodicals and collaborated with his friend Robert Louis Stevenson. He was also the joint compiler of a slang dictionary. He wrote criticism as well as poetry, and edited anthologies. He died in 1903.

Robert Herrick 35

Born in Cheapside in 1591, the son of a goldsmith. His father died after falling out of a window. The widow and her eight children moved to Hampton-on-Thames. Herrick probably went to Westminster School till he was sixteen, when he was apprenticed to an uncle who was a goldsmith. At twenty-one he went to Cambridge. He became a parson and was sent to the parish of Dean Prior near Plymouth. Little is known of his life there, save that he kept a pet pig and once threw his sermon at the heads of his congregation. He felt exiled in Devon and eventually returned to London, but it was at Dean Prior that he wrote his loveliest lyrics. He died in 1674.

Ralph Hodgson   46

Born in Yorkshire in 1871. He worked as a journalist and draughtsman in Fleet Street. In 1924 he was appointed lecturer on English Literature at Sendai University, Japan, and now lives in America. Besides being a man of letters he is a leading authority on bull terriers and waged a campaign to end the docking of their tails and the clipping of their ears.

James Hogg   46

Born in 1770, son of a poor farmer in Selkirk. When he first started writing down his verses he could only get down about six lines at a time because the labour of writing was so great. In 1790 he went as shepherd to a farm in Yarrow, and got as his next job that of steward for Sir Walter Scott. In 1801 he collected his poems and had them published in Edinburgh, and nine years later decided to try and make his way by his pen. He made a name for himself as 'The Ettrick Shepherd' in Edinburgh, and was helped by Lord Byron and others who eventually established him on a farm of his own. He wrote and published verse and essays till his death in 1835.

Gerard Manley Hopkins   13, 69, 89, 171, 203

Born in 1844, educated at Highgate and Balliol College, Oxford. He became a Roman Catholic when he was twenty-two and afterwards a Jesuit priest. He was a friend of Robert Bridges with whom he corresponded and to whom he entrusted his work. His poems were not published till after his death in 1889. He wrote: 'No doubt my poetry errs on the side of oddness . . . but take breath and read it with the ears, as I always wish to be read, and my verse becomes alright.'

A. E. Housman   35, 82, 90

Born in Shropshire in 1859. Educated at Bromsgrove School and St John's College, Oxford. He was a distinguished classical scholar and became a Professor of Latin at London and Cambridge. As well as being a scholar he was editor and poet. He published numerous articles in classical journals and edited editions of Juvenal and Lucan. His first book of poems, *The Shropshire Lad*, was published in 1896 and *Last Poems* in 1922. He died in 1936.

Richard Hovey 74

Born at Normal, Illinois, in 1864, he spent his boyhood in Washington. He published his first book of verse when he was sixteen; he learned to set the type himself, and had printed, bound, and copyrighted the book before his parents knew anything about it. He died in 1900.

Richard Hughes 5, 47, 119

Born in 1900. Educated at Charterhouse and Oxford. A Welshman by blood, he lives with his wife and five children in a lonely white house on the shore of Cardigan Bay. He has written plays, novels (*A High Wind in Jamaica*, the story of a family of children who are prisoners on a pirate schooner, became well known), poetry, and stories for boys and girls. The poems reprinted here come from *Confessio Juvenis*, first published in 1926.

Aldous Huxley 151

Born in 1894. Grandson of the Victorian scientist and brother of Dr Julian Huxley. Educated at Eton and Balliol College, Oxford. His first volume of short stories was published in 1920, followed by several gay, frivolous novels. He has published work of many kinds; poetry, plays, essays, biography, philosophy, criticism. In the late nineteen-thirties he moved to California where he now lives.

Jean Ingelow 267

Born in 1820 in Boston, Lincolnshire. Daughter of a banker with a Scots wife. She was brought up very strictly and educated at home. In 1863 she went to London. She published poems and stories for girls. She was a friend of Tennyson, Ruskin, Browning, and Christina Rossetti. Her poems were very highly thought of while she was alive. She died in Kensington in 1897.

Ben Jonson 20

Born in Westminster in 1572, a month after his father's death. He started work as an actor in 1597, but found he had no talent so took to writing plays. His first play, *Every Man in His Humour*, was performed at the Globe Theatre with William Shakespeare as one of the cast. Once he killed a fellow actor in a duel and escaped the gallows but had all his goods confiscated and a brand put on his right thumb. He was notoriously sensitive and quarrelsome. Much of his poetry has been lost. His best-known plays are *Volpone*, *The Silent Woman*, and *The Alchemist*. He died in 1637.

John Keats

Born in 1795, he was the middle one of three brothers and had a younger sister. His father worked in a livery stables. John was apprenticed to a surgeon but became ill and never finished his training. He travelled in search of health, but died when he was twenty-six in Rome. The verses *A Song about Myself* were written in a letter to Fanny Keats, his beloved sister.

Charles Kingsley

Born in 1819 at Holne Vicarage on Dartmoor, the eldest and most famous of three author sons of the Rev Charles Kingsley. Educated at Clifton, at the Grammar School at Helston, and at Magdalene College, Cambridge. He became a clergyman and was given a parish on the outskirts of Windsor Forest. He wrote sermons, lectures, and adventure stories (like *Westward Ho!*) and in 1863 *The Water Babies*. He also wrote a quantity of verse. He became Professor of Modern History at Cambridge. He died at Eversley in Hampshire in 1875.

Rudyard Kipling

Born 1865 in Bombay. Educated at the United Services College at Westward Ho! (the background of *Stalky & Co*). His holidays were spent in Kensington High Street in the care of three dear ladies in a house full of books. 'Somewhere in the background were people called Jean Ingelow and Christina Rossetti, but I was never lucky enough to see these good spirits.' He went back to India and worked there as a journalist till 1889. His first novel was *The Light That Failed*. *The Jungle Books* were written when he left India and lived for a time in New England. He settled in Sussex where he died in 1936.

D. H. Lawrence

Born in 1885, the son of a miner, in Eastwood, Nottinghamshire. Educated at Nottingham High School and University College, Nottingham. Married in 1914. He started as a teacher in Croydon, but soon devoted himself to writing. He travelled widely through Italy, New Mexico, and Australia. He wrote short stories, essays, novels, and poetry. A volume of his letters has been published. He died of consumption in 1930 and is buried in Vence in the south of France where his grave is marked by a phoenix carved in stone by a peasant who had become his friend.

Edward Lear

Born in Highgate in 1812, the youngest of a family of twenty-one children. He was trained as a painter, was commissioned to do detailed illustrations of animals and birds, and travelled widely painting landscapes. He kept long diaries and wrote innumerable letters. It always surprised him that 'such an assinine beetle' could have made so many friends. At one time he was art master to Queen Victoria. He is said to be 'the father of the limerick'. He lived mainly on the Italian Riviera with his Albanian servant and his cat Foss. He died at San Remo in 1888.

Francis Ledwidge

Born in 1891 in County Meath. The fifth child of an evicted tenant famer. He was educated at Slane National School until he was twelve, then he worked as a farm labourer, domestic servant, grocer's apprentice, and ganger on the roads. He sent his notebook full of verses to Lord Dunsany who encouraged him. He fought in the First World War and was killed in Belgium in 1917. He has been called the Burns and Clare of Ireland. His first book *Songs of the Field* was published in 1915; his complete poems with a preface by Lord Dunsany in 1919.

Alun Lewis

Born in 1915 in a mining district in South Wales. He wrote short stories, mainly about his experiences in the South Wales Borderers which he joined at the beginning of the 1939 war. His poetry has been published in two volumes, *Ha! Ha! Among the Trumpets* and *Raiders' Dawn*. In 1944 he was killed in an accident in India.

Cecil Day Lewis

Born in Ireland in 1904. He was educated at Sherborne and Wadham College, Oxford. He has been a schoolmaster at Oxford, Helensburgh, and Cheltenham. During the war he was in the Home Guard in Devon (the poem *The Watching Post* describes a night duty in the Axe valley), and later at the Ministry of Information. He is poet, novelist, lecturer, and broadcaster. He was recently elected Professor of Poetry at Oxford. He writes detective stories under a pseudonym, and has written two books specially for boys and girls, *The Otterbury Incident* (an adventure story), and *Poetry for You*.

Eiluned Lewis   67

Born in Montgomeryshire of Welsh parents. She worked in Fleet Street on the editorial staffs of the *News Chronicle* and the *Sunday Times*. In 1936 she married and has one daughter. Her first novel *Dew on the Grass* about a family of children growing up in the country was awarded the Book Guild Gold Medal for 1934. She contributes regularly to *Country Life* and has published two books of verse.

Henry Wadsworth Longfellow   158, 235

Born in 1807 in Portland, Maine, the son of a lawyer. He became a Professor of Modern Languages at Harvard University. He became widely known for a great deal of popular verse like *Hiawatha* and *The Wreck of the Hesperus*. He died in 1882.

Lilian Bowes Lyon   29, 185, 264

Born in 1895 in Northumberland and, although she lived and worked subsequently in many places, always remained devoted to that tough northern countryside. She went to no school but spent eighteen months at Oxford. She published two novels, and six separate books make up her *Collected Poems*. During the last war she worked in the East End during the raids and received injuries that made her a cripple till her death in 1949.

Lord Macaulay   250

Thomas Babington, Lord Macaulay, was born in 1800 at Rothley Temple, Leicestershire. He was a very precocious child, who seemed to come into the world already grown up. From the time that he was three he read incessantly, 'prone on his stomach in front of the fire, his book on the hearthrug and a piece of bread and butter in his hand'. He was educated at Shelford and Cambridge. He became an eminent historian who wrote his 'Lays' as relaxation. They were hated by Matthew Arnold, but Francis Thompson used to carry a copy of them in his pocket for comfort when he was at school. He died in Kensington in 1859.

Rose Macaulay   22

A descendant of Lord Macaulay. Brought up in Italy by the sea, she was one of a large cheerful family who enjoyed bathing, paddling, and canoeing. 'I went in largely for roof climbing and other mischievous activities. I was very fond of hockey, tennis and boating.' She has published two volumes of verse but is best known for her many, mainly satirical, novels. She first began to write a novel with her sister when she was three, under a table. She recently travelled down the Mediterranean coast of Spain by herself in a car and wrote a book about it called *Fabled Shore*.

Louis Macneice   123

Born in 1907 in Belfast. Son of the Bishop of Down, Connor, and Dromore. Educated at Marlborough and Merton College, Oxford. Lecturer in classics at Birmingham University 1930, then lecturer in Greek at Bedford College, London. Since 1941 he has worked at the B.B.C. and many of his radio plays and feature programmes have been broadcast. In 1929 he published a book of poems but his first serious work appeared in *Poems* in 1935. He has now published five volumes of verse as well as travel books, a poetic drama, a study of Yeats, and a collection of radio plays.

Andrew Marvell   40, 141

Born in 1621 in Yorkshire, the son of a vicar. Later his father became Headmaster of Hull Grammar School, and Marvell was educated there. He went on to Trinity College, Cambridge, then travelled in Holland, France, Italy, and Spain, and learned the languages of all these countries. His first poems were published in Greek and Latin. He became a tutor, a Member of Parliament, and secretary to the Earl of Carlisle during his embassies to Russia and Scandinavia. He published pamphlets which were highly praised by Swift, many miscellaneous writings, and poetry. He died of malaria in 1668.

John Masefield 74, 75, 237

Born in 1878, his parents died when he was a boy. He was brought up by an aunt, but ran away to sea when he was fourteen. He lived for two years in America working at odd jobs (in a bakery, livery stable, carpet factory, saloon), and on his return to England was attached to the staff of the *Manchester Guardian*. His first book, *Salt-water Ballads*, was published in 1902. During the First World War he served with the Red Cross in France and at Gallipoli. He was made Poet Laureate in 1930 on the death of Robert Bridges. He settled near Oxford, where he did his writing (according to Robert Graves who once rented a cottage at the bottom of his garden), 'in a hut surrounded by gorse bushes, only appearing for meals'. In 1935 he was awarded the Order of Merit.

Irene McLeod 177

Began writing verse before she was seven and has continued to do so all her life. She has published five volumes of verse, two novels, and *Six o'clock and After*, a volume of verse for children in collaboration with her husband, Aubrey de Selincourt. She has given broadcast talks on birds and has written plays for the B.B.C.'s Children's Hour. She originally trained for the stage and was an actress before her marriage. She has two daughters. This poem, *The Lone Dog*, was composed in her sleep and remembered completely on waking.

Charlotte Mew 47, 205

Born in 1870 in London, the daughter of an architect whose early death left his family in financial difficulties. She passed the whole of her life, save for short intervals, in the heart of Bloomsbury. Friends talked of her 'deep charm and wit'. She had a great dislike of personal publicity and put every obstacle in its way. She was always poor, but was helped just before her death by a Civil List Pension. On the death of her mother and sister she committed suicide in a nursing home in 1928. Her poems were published in two volumes, *The Farmer's Bride* and *Sailor's Garland*.

Alice Meynell 62, 111, 198

Born in 1847 in London and spent her youth in Italy. She married Wilfred Meynell, the editor and publisher, and had seven children. In a house full of family and friends and books, she contrived to write essays, criticism, and poetry. She was friend and inspiration to Francis Thompson. She died in 1922.

William Miller 88

Born in Glasgow in 1810, he was apprenticed to a wood-turner and became a skilled craftsman. In 1863 he published *Nursery Songs and other Poems* and became known as 'The Laureate of the Nursery'. He died in 1872.

Harold Monro 70, 151

Born in 1879. Educated at Radley and Caius College, Cambridge. He travelled widely, and, not content with writing poetry, also promoted it by starting The Poetry Bookshop. He published and sold the first works of little-known poets who afterwards became famous. He was a Londoner who wrote about the country, seeing it with the intense loving eye of the week-ender. He died in 1932.

Thomas Moore 85

Born in Dublin in 1779, the son of a grocer. He was educated privately and at Trinity College, Dublin. He won his way into society by his good looks and charming manner. He travelled to Bermuda, where he had an appointment as admiralty registrar, but delegated this to someone else, and travelled farther, through the United States and Canada. He became a friend of Lord Byron, and wrote a *Life of Byron* after his death. He made his name as a poet with a long poem on an eastern subject—rather in the manner of Byron—*Lalla Rookh*. He died in 1852.

Thomas Sturge Moore 105

Born at Hastings in 1870, the son of a physician. He left school at the age of fourteen because of ill health and gave as much time to the study of art as of literature. He published volumes of verse and produced a number of wood engravings of his own design. In 1920 he was granted a Civil List Pension. He died in 1944.

Born in 1893. Educated at Harrow and Oxford. He fought in the
First World War and began journalism as a reporter and weekly
poet on the *Sunday Express*. Since 1924 he has been 'Beachcomber' of
the *Daily Express*. He has published more than forty books, ranging
from the humorous to serious historical studies. His own favourites
among his books are a travel book, *Pyranean*, and *The Death of the
Dragon*, a volume of fairy stories. It is as a humorist that he is most
widely known, and the public school Narkover that he created is
now world famous.

Edwin Muir   186

Born in 1887 in the Orkney Islands. Educated at Kirkwall Burgh
School. At fourteen he became a clerk in a commercial and ship-
building firm in Glasgow. He married in 1919 and settled mainly
in London although he has travelled widely on the Continent. He
has published work as a journalist, poet, critic, novelist, and
translator.

Ogden Nash   228, 241

Born in 1902 in the United States. Educated at St George's
School, Newport, R.I. and at Harvard University. He worked in
a publisher's office until so much of his work was printed in so
many magazines that he became well known as a humorous poet.
His first books of verse were published in 1931, *Hard Lines* and
Free Wheeling. His work has been judged 'the best light verse
written in America today'. He is married and has two daughters,
Linell and Isabel.

E. Nesbit   95

Born in London in 1858, the youngest of a family of six. Her
father died when she was a child. She was sent to school in France
and spent holidays in Kent. She began writing for magazines when
she was eighteen. Married Hubert Bland who lost his money in
some unlucky investments so, in order to support the family,
his wife worked at painting Christmas cards, as a public reciter, at
literary hack work, and as a poet. In 1899 she wrote *The Treasure*

Seekers, which was an immediate success. For her five children she continued the history of the Bastable family in books that are still popular today. She died in 1924.

Robert Nichols

Born in 1893 in Essex. Educated at Winchester and Trinity College, Oxford. He served in the army on the Western Front in the First World War. His first poems, *Invocation,* were published in 1915. A last selection from his work, *Such Was My Singing,* appeared in 1942. He married in 1922, and was for a time Professor of English Literature in the Imperial University, Tokyo. He died in Cambridge in 1944.

Alfred Noyes

Born in Wolverhampton in 1880 and brought up by the sea. He went to Exeter College, Oxford, where he was in the college rowing eight. *The Loom of Years* was his first volume of poetry, published when he was twenty-two. George Meredith encouraged him and praised his early work. He has written plays, biographies, essays, short stories, and for a time was a lecturer in America. Mainly he has spent his life in writing poetry. He is married, lives on the Isle of Wight, and has a son and two daughters.

Wilfred Owen

Born in 1893 at Plas Wilmot, Oswestry. Educated at Birkenhead Institute and the University of London. He went as tutor to a family in Bordeaux and spent a holiday in the Pyrenees, which was when this poem was written. When the First World War broke out he enlisted in the Artists' Rifles and was gazetted to the Manchester Regiment. He won the M.C., then was killed by machine-gun fire on 4 November 1918.

Clement Paman

This carol was written in 1660 or thereabouts. Of the author there is nothing to relate. The poem was found by Norman Ault (British Museum Manuscript Add. 18220) and reproduced in his *A Treasury of Unfamiliar Lyrics,* 1938.

Thomas Love Peacock

Born at Weymouth in 1785. Son of a London merchant. He was self-educated. For most of his life he was employed in the India Office. He was one of Shelley's closest friends and his executor. His daughter married George Meredith. He wrote satirical romances and verses. He died in 1866.

Ruth Pitter 31, 52, 162, 163, 199, 273

Born in 1897 at Ilford in Essex, the daughter of a schoolmaster. She went to elementary and secondary schools and took her first job at the War Office during the First World War. When invalided out she wanted to be some kind of artist, so learnt the making and decorating of furniture and other things. From this she has made a living that enabled her to write poetry at the same time. She began writing at the age of five, and was first published in *The New Age* in 1910. In 1937 she won the Hawthornden Prize for *A Trophy of Arms*, her first mature book of serious poems. She has never written very much but her work has appeared in nine small volumes.

John Pudney

Born in the Thames Valley in 1909. He was at preparatory school in Kent and then went on to Gresham's School, Holt. He served in the R.A.F. during the war and made a name with his poems about aircrews, *Dispersal Point*, and *Beyond this Disregard*. He has published novels, essays, radio and film scripts, poetry and country books. His *Fred and I* adventure stories for boys and girls have been broadcast and published.

James Reeves 99, 224, 225

Born in 1909. He began writing poems when he was eleven. He grew up in the country and was educated at Stowe and Cambridge. He is married and has two daughters and a son. He has travelled widely in Europe. Is now a critic and broadcaster, and lives opposite Milton's cottage in Chalfont St Giles. He has published several volumes of poems, two for children, *The Blackbird in the Lilac* and *The Wandering Moon*.

Michael Roberts

Born in Bournemouth in 1902, educated at King's College, London, and Trinity College, Cambridge. He was a schoolmaster in Newcastle and joined the B.B.C. European Service during the war. He became editor of broadcasts for the underground papers in Europe and contributed articles to them. He published three volumes of verse and many volumes of criticism, and was editor of *The Faber Book of Modern Verse*. He died in 1948.

W. R. Rodgers

Born in Ulster in 1909, educated at Queen's University, Belfast. For twelve years he was a clergyman in Co. Armagh, then resigned his parish and joined the B.B.C. features department. Since 1946 he has been producer and script writer. His first book of verse, *Awake, and Other Poems*, was published in 1941 and was praised as the most promising first book of poetry since W. H. Auden's *Poems*. In 1951 he was elected to the Irish Academy of Letters to fill the vacancy caused by the death of Bernard Shaw.

Christina Georgina Rossetti

Born in 1830, the daughter of an Italian patriot who came to England in 1824. Sister of Dante Gabriel Rossetti. Under a pseudonym wrote poems which she contributed to the magazine started by the Pre-Raphaelite Brotherhood (Holman Hunt, Dante Gabriel, Millais, and others), *The Germ*. Published her first volume of poems, *Goblin Market*, in 1862. Many other volumes followed this. She died in 1894.

Vita Sackville-West

Born in 1892 at Knole, near Sevenoaks, a descendant of Thomas Sackville who was given Knole Castle by Queen Elizabeth. Her husband is Sir Harold Nicholson. They have two sons and now live in Kent at Sissinghurst Castle. She is novelist as well as poet. She has travelled in Persia, Hungary, Bulgaria, and Morocco, and is a skilful gardener. In 1927 *The Land* won the Hawthornden Prize. Sir Hugh Walpole wrote of her, 'She has done everything in life . . . simply because she thought it would be a delightful thing to do.'

Siegfried Sassoon   31, 33, 189, 214

Born in 1886, educated at Marlborough and Clare College, Cambridge. He fought in the First World War and has described his experiences in his autobiographical books and semi-biographical novels. *The Memoirs of a Foxhunting Man* won the Hawthornden Prize and the James Tait Black Memorial Prize. He was a journalist in London after the First World War, then moved to the country to be husband, father, poet, writer, and Master of Foxhounds.

Sir Walter Scott   40

Born in 1771 in Edinburgh, the son of a lawyer. He began a legal career and was called to the Bar. When he was twenty-one a slim volume of his verse translations was published. When he was thirty-four he published *The Lay of the Last Minstrel*, and became established as a successful poet. He built a vast home, Abbotsford, for himself and his family, in the border country. Difficulties with his publisher and the expense of his building project led him into debt. It was to get out of difficulties that he turned to writing novels. From 1814 onwards he wrote the Waverley Novels, which included only incidental lyrics. He was offered, and turned down, the post of Poet Laureate. In 1820 he was knighted. Byron wrote to his publisher: 'I shall think higher of the knighthood ever after for his being dubbed.' He was the first poet titled for his talent in Britain. He died in 1832.

Ian Serraillier   164, 222

Born in 1912 in London. Son of a French father and Scottish mother. Educated at Brighton College and St Edmund Hall, Oxford. He has been a schoolmaster since 1935. His main interest is writing for children in verse and prose. His first book of verse, *The Weaver Birds*, was published in 1944. He has published three more since then, as well as adventure stories. His tales in verse have been broadcast. He and his large family live in Sussex but spend holidays abroad when possible. He has canoed 250 miles down the Danube and climbed and ski'd in the Alps.

Edward Shanks   107, 114

Born in 1892. Educated at Merchant Taylors and Trinity College, Cambridge. He became novelist, essayist, poet and literary journalist. He was one of the best known 'Georgian' poets in the early twenties. His belief was that poetry must be 'a singing'. He died in 1953.

Percy Bysshe Shelley 41

Born in 1792, the eldest of seven children of a country squire. His boyhood was spent in Sussex. Educated at Sion House, Eton, and University College, Oxford. He was expelled from his college for the publication of a pamphlet on *The Necessity of Atheism*. As a youth he lived in rooms in London, kept from starvation by his sisters who sent him their pocket money. He married twice and in 1818 took his family to Italy where he eventually settled at Lerici on the Gulf of Spezzia. His first major poem *Alastor* was published in 1816 and other works appeared at frequent intervals till his death in 1822. 'An unforgettable being of lyric genius', he was drowned when the boat he was sailing was run down by a felucca in a storm.

Sir Osbert Sitwell 102

Born in 1892. Fifth Baronet. Of school at Eton he writes 'hated [it] passionately and still do'. He was in the Grenadier Guards from 1913 to 1919. He has written more prose than poetry (his sister Edith Sitwell is the chief poet of the family), essays, short stories, novels, and an autobiography in four volumes. His younger brother Sacheverell Sitwell has called him 'the most brilliant conversationalist since Oscar Wilde'.

Martyn Skinner 252

Born in Acton in 1906. Educated at Magdalen College, Oxford. He is married, is a farmer in Oxfordshire, and has two sons and one daughter. The *Letters to Malaya* were written from England to a friend in Malaya during the war. They appeared in three volumes, the second of which was awarded the Hawthornden Prize. They form a witty commentary on the contemporary world. The poet's recreations are letter-writing, kite-flying, and local government.

Christopher Smart 203

Born in Kent in 1722. Educated at Maidstone and Durham and Pembroke College, Cambridge. His first publication was some verses in Latin, and he wrote also *A Trip to Cambridge* which was acted in college. He was made a Fellow, but got into debt and was imprisoned in his rooms by his creditors. In London he worked as the editor of various magazines for women, using a pseudonym. He also wrote verse for advertisements, and published poems and translations. He married and had two daughters, but was separated from his family. He had bouts of insanity, during one of which he wrote his only great work, *The Song to David*. This was highly praised by both Browning and Rossetti. He died in an asylum in 1771.

C. Fox Smith   128, 156

Born in Yorkshire, she began to write at a very early age. Her first book was published when she was sixteen. She collected much of her knowledge of ships and sailors on the Pacific coast when there were still square-rigged sailing vessels to be seen, and later in and about the London Docks. She published several volumes of verse, mainly about the sea, and novels for boys and girls. She contributed verse, essays, and poems to many periodicals, including *Punch*, and lived in Devon until her death in 1954.

Robert Southwell   257

Born in 1561 at Horsham St Faith's in Norfolk. He was stolen from his cradle by gipsies because he was such a beautiful child, but he was returned. Educated at Douai and in Paris. In 1584 he became a Jesuit priest. He came to England during the persecution of the Roman Catholic Church and survived for six years. He travelled as missionary all over the country and was private chaplain to Lady Arundel. At last he was caught, imprisoned in the Tower of London, and executed at Tyburn in 1595. Most of his poems were written while he was a prisoner.

Stephen Spender   147

Born in 1909. Educated at University College School and University College, Oxford. At Oxford he was a contemporary of W. H. Auden and Louis Macneice. He has travelled widely in Europe; lived for some time in Germany and was in Spain during the Civil War. He has published several volumes of poetry, short stories, criticism, a novel, and an autobiography, *World Within World*.

James Stephens

Born in Dublin in 1882. He was 'discovered' by the poet 'Æ' (G. W. Russell) working in a lawyer's office as a typist. It was 'Æ' who encouraged him to become a writer and poet. His best-known book is *The Crock of Gold* which was written in shorthand notebooks and when eventually published won a literary prize. His first book of verse, *Insurrection*, was published in 1909. He lived the last years of his life in London, and became more widely known than ever before through his occasional broadcasts. He died in 1951.

Robert Louis Stevenson

Born in 1850 in Edinburgh, son of a civil engineer. He studied engineering at Edinburgh University but switched to Law and in 1875 was called to the Scottish Bar. He was dogged by bad health all his life and travelled constantly to find relief. *An Inland Voyage* and *Travels With a Donkey* are the first two books that made him known. Later he wrote stories, travel books, essays, and poems. He went to California in 1879, and married a Mrs Osborne. It was for his stepson Lloyd Osborne that he wrote *Treasure Island*. During the last years of his life he lived on the island of Samoa in the South Seas. He died there in 1894.

Thomas Tod Stoddart

Born in Edinburgh in 1810 and educated at the university there. His main interest in life was angling and, when he went to live near Kelso, he fished in the Tweed and Teviot. He wrote books on angling, and is remembered as the Scottish Isaak Walton. His book of verses, *The Death-Wake*, was published when he was twenty-one, but went unnoticed till it was discovered and praised by Andrew Lang sixty years later.

Sir Rabindranath Tagore

Born in Calcutta in 1861. He began to write verse at the age of eight. When he was seventeen he came to England with the idea of studying Law, but abandoned this and wrote poetry instead. Contemporaries called him 'the Bengal Shelley'. When his father died he went back to India to look after the family estates. He founded a famous school in Bengal. In 1913 he was awarded a Nobel Prize, and was knighted two years later. He died in 1941.

Alfred, Lord Tennyson

Born in 1809, the son of the Rector of Somersby in Lincolnshire. He went to Louth Grammar School and Trinity College, Cambridge. It was there that he became a friend of Arthur Hallam, upon whose death he wrote *In Memoriam*. He won the Chancellor's Medal for a poem called *Timbuctoo* and published his first volume of poems when he was twenty-one. He was engaged for seventeen years before his marriage in 1850. In the same year he was made Poet Laureate in succession to Wordsworth. In 1884 he was created a Baron and when he died in 1892 he was buried in Westminster Abbey.

A. S. J. Tessimond

Born in Birkenhead in 1902. Educated at Charterhouse and Liverpool University. He has been schoolmaster, bookseller, and copywriter in an advertising agency. His poems have been published in *Penguin New Writing*, *Horizon*, and *The Listener*. They have also been collected into a volume published under the title *The Walls of Glass*.

Edward Thomas

Born 1878. Educated at St Paul's School and Lincoln College, Oxford. He married while still at the university. They lived at first in lodgings in London and later in a cottage in Sussex. He was determined to support his family by writing, and struggled with much hackwork, biography, essays, topography. Perhaps his best prose books are *Richard Jefferies* and *Light and Twilight*. He was a friend of Rupert Brooke, Wilfred Gibson, Arthur Ransome, Eleanor Farjeon, and Walter de la Mare. It was Robert Frost who first suggested that he should write poetry, which he started to do when he joined the Artists' Rifles at the beginning of the First World War. He was killed at Arras in 1917.

Francis Thompson

Born in 1859 in Ashton, Lancashire. He was the son of a doctor and intended to study medicine but lost interest and made his way to London. He lived there on the streets and in doss-houses, a penniless poet and dreamer. He was helped by Wilfred and Alice Meynell who placed his prose work and arranged for his poems to be published. They supported him financially and with their encouragement. He was always an unsettled wanderer, a fervent

Catholic, unsatisfactory from any practical point of view, but a real poet. He died of tuberculosis in 1907.

Thomas Traherne   8, 25, 192

Born about 1634, a shoemaker's son from Hereford. He was educated at Brasenose College, Oxford, became domestic chaplain to Sir Orlando Bridgeman, at Teddington, near Hampton Court. It was there that he lived for the rest of his life, a gentle, devout man. Only one book of his was published during his lifetime. After his death in 1674 friends collected and published two volumes of his verse and prose. Other manuscripts were passed from hand to hand until their discovery and publication at the beginning of this century.

Herbert Trevelyan   92

Herbert Trevelyan is a fictitious name, and the author's true name is not known. A memoir by 'Mrs Dorothy Potts' describes how Mr Trevelyan, a beautiful but melancholy young man who lodged in her cottage at Windermere, would row on the lake, or sit and sigh in the churchyard, and how he became ill, paid what he owed her, and died.

W. J. Turner   79, 140

Born in 1889 in Melbourne, Australia. He came to Europe in 1910. He was a writer and editor on many subjects, particularly music and ballet. During the war he edited the Britain in Pictures series of books. He published many volumes of poetry. He died in 1946.

Arthur Waley   94, 101, 113, 189, 213

Born in 1889 at Tunbridge Wells. Educated at Rugby and King's College, Canterbury. He is our greatest living authority on Chinese language and literature. He has published many volumes of translations from the Chinese, particularly *Monkey*, a Chinese novel, and *170 Chinese Poems*. Although the original Chinese poems have rhyme, this is lost in the translations though many of the rhythms remain.

Mary Webb   37, 78, 83

Born at Leighton, a small village in Shropshire, in 1881. Her father was of Welsh descent; her mother the daughter of an Edinburgh doctor. In 1912 she married. She lived, except for one or two short intervals, in Shropshire all her life and that county forms the background of her six novels. These brought her many admirers.

Walter de la Mare describes her 'bright blue eyes, fair brown hair, small hands; bird-like, demure. She loved to listen to others talking as much as to talk herself, but her own talk had an extraordinary eagerness and vivacity'. She died in 1921.

Dorothy Wellesley

Duchess of Wellington. Born at Croughton, Cheshire. Married Lord Gerald Wellesley and had one son and one daughter. She travelled widely and was the friend and benefactor of many poets and writers. Her own publications included biographies, critical works, and poems. She was editor of the Hogarth Living Poets series, lived in Kent, and published a volume of autobiography, *Far Have I Travelled*. She died in 1956.

Thomas Westwood

Born in Enfield in 1814, the son of an eccentric retired haberdasher who was a friend of Charles Lamb. He browsed in Lamb's library when he was a boy. In 1840 his first volume of poems was published. He accepted a position in a Belgian Railway Company, and spent the rest of his life in Belgium. His great hobby was collecting books on fishing. He died in 1884.

Walt Whitman

Born on Long Island in 1819, the son of a farmer. When he was thirteen he worked in a printing office, when twenty-one he was an editor. During the American Civil War he helped to nurse the wounded. He designed his poetry as a break away from the traditions of Europe, wanting to make a new poetic language to suit the new American world. When *Leaves of Grass* was published in 1855 it was violently criticized and loudly praised. He published many further books of verse, and died in 1892.

Charles Williams

Born in London in 1886. He was educated at St Albans Grammar School and University College, London. For thirty-six years he worked as an editor for the Oxford University Press. During this time he wrote novels, criticism, and poetry. During the last war he was a lecturer and private tutor at Oxford. He died in 1945.

X 2

Born in 1885 in Milan. Educated at Bedford Grammar School and Wadham College, Oxford. In 1908 he entered the Civil Service. By day he was a Civil Servant, by night a poet. He became Deputy secretary of the Ministry of Labour and at the same time published poems and critical essays. He wrote some poetic fantasies that were performed in London. His first book was published in 1915, and his last, *Kensington Gardens in Wartime*, in 1940. He died in that year.

William Wordsworth 59, 83, 89, 155

Born at Cockermouth in Cumberland in 1770. One of a family of three brothers and a sister whose parents died when they were children. He was educated at local schools and at St John's College, Cambridge. He travelled on the Continent before settling with his sister in a cottage in Somerset for two years and then in the Lake District. She became his devoted companion and housekeeper and continued to live with him after his marriage to Mary Hutchinson, their mutual friend. He was a friend of Coleridge, with whom he designed the *Lyrical Ballads*. He died at Rydal in 1850.

W. B. Yeats 48, 127, 176, 178

Born at Sandymount in Ireland in 1865. Educated at the Godolphin School, Hammersmith, and in Dublin. He studied art and concentrated on painting for three years before turning to literature. His first poems were published in 1889. He helped to establish the Irish National Theatre. In 1923 he was awarded a Nobel Prize. From 1927 to 1928 he was a senator in the Irish Free State. He lived with his wife and two children in an ancient tower on the coast of Ireland. In 1939 he died in the south of France, but his ashes were taken back to Ireland after the war.

Andrew Young 69, 120, 171, 260, 266

Born in Elgin in 1885, he went to Edinburgh University and is now Vicar of Stonegate, Sussex, and Canon of Chichester Cathedral. He used to play truant from school and although he hated the country was driven to seek refuge there and became interested in wild flowers. He is now an authority on these and has written two books about them. His *Collected Poems* were published in 1948.

Index of First Lines

How happy is the little stone, 206.

I am fevered with the sunset, 74.
I am the sun's remembrancer, the boy, 84.
I arose early, O my true love! 31.
I asked of Night, that she would take me, 21.
I can imagine, in some other world, 173.
I cannot tell what you say, green leaves, 197.
I dance and sing without any feet—, 224.
If all the world were paper, 223.
If there were dreams to sell, 19.
If trees were tall and grasses short, 20.
If you can catch a leaf, so they say, 99.
I have a garden of my own, 85.
I have a horse—a ryghte goode horse, 223.
I have wished a bird would fly away, 172.
I heard a bird at dawn, 32.
I heard a horseman, 8.
I know a Room where tulips tall, 217.
I long to go over there to the further bank of the river, 50.
I love the stillness of the wood, 56.
I'm a lean dog, a keen dog, a wild dog, and lone, 177.
In autumn down the beechwood path, 99.
I never saw a lovelier sky, 266.
I never went to Mamble, 144.
In the least flowering weed she lies, 199.
In the middle of countries, far from hills and sea, 151.
In the wild October night-time, when the wind raved round the
    land, 251.
I ran over a pig, 227.
Isabel met an enormous bear, 241.
I saw a frieze on whitest marble drawn, 79.
I saw a man on a horse, 188.
I saw a ship a-sailing, a-sailing, a-sailing, 75.
I sometimes think I'd rather crow, 228.
I think they were about as high, 47.
It is May, it is May! 92.
It's ten years ago today you turned me out o' doors, 187.
It was a perfect day, 264.
It was the time when lilies blow, 94.
I was reared, 66.

311

Index of Titles

PRINTED IN GREAT BRITAIN
AT THE UNIVERSITY PRESS, OXFORD
BY VIVIAN RIDLER
PRINTER TO THE UNIVERSITY